REAPING THE BENEFITS OF INDUSTRY 4.0 THROUGH SKILLS DEVELOPMENT IN INDONESIA

JANUARY 2021

ASIAN DEVELOPMENT BANK

ADB

© 2021 Asian Development Bank
6 ADB Avenue, Mandaluyong City, 1550 Metro Manila, Philippines
Tel +63 2 8632 4444; Fax +63 2 8636 2444
www.adb.org

Some rights reserved. Published in 2021.

ISBN 978-92-9262-452-1 (print); 978-92-9262-453-8 (electronic); 978-92-9262-454-5 (ebook)
Publication Stock No. SPR200327
DOI: http://dx.doi.org/10.22617/SPR200327

The views expressed in this publication are those of the authors and do not necessarily reflect the views and policies of the Asian Development Bank (ADB) or its Board of Governors or the governments they represent.

ADB does not guarantee the accuracy of the data included in this publication and accepts no responsibility for any consequence of their use. The mention of specific companies or products of manufacturers does not imply that they are endorsed or recommended by ADB in preference to others of a similar nature that are not mentioned.

By making any designation of or reference to a particular territory or geographic area, or by using the term "country" in this document, ADB does not intend to make any judgments as to the legal or other status of any territory or area.

Corrigenda to ADB publications may be found at http://www.adb.org/publications/corrigenda.

Notes:
In this publication, "$" refers to United States dollars.
ADB recognizes "China" as the People's Republic of China.

Cover design by Mike Cortes.

Contents

iii

Tables, Figures, and Boxes

Boxes

Foreword

Talent and skills are valuable in powering knowledge-based economies. The Fourth Industrial Revolution (4IR) has ushered in extraordinary technological advances, fusing boundaries of physical, digital, and biological worlds to create new paradigms in the way we live, work, and interact. These trends have heralded excitement and fear—excitement in advancing frontiers of human endeavor and fear of negative repercussions on jobs and rising inequalities.

To respond to questions and concerns in developing member countries of the Asian Development Bank (ADB) on how their economies can transition effectively to 4IR, the study *"Reaping the Benefits of Industry 4.0 Through Skills Development in High-Growth Industries in Southeast Asia"* builds an evidence based on opportunities, challenges, and promising approaches in 4IR. It covers Cambodia, Indonesia, the Philippines, and Viet Nam with specific focus on two industries in each country deemed important for growth, employment, and 4IR: tourism and garments in Cambodia, food and beverage manufacturing and automotive manufacturing in Indonesia, information technology and business process outsourcing and electronics in the Philippines, and agro-processing and logistics in Viet Nam.

Much has been written about anticipated loss of millions of jobs arising from automation. At ADB, we take a tempered view. The study reaffirms a positive outlook to 4IR creating new opportunities for quality jobs. While many jobs will indeed be lost as a result of automation, new jobs will emerge through the adoption of technologies that will increase worker productivity and competitiveness of nations, thereby leading to greater prosperity. However, tapping such benefits is predicated on increasing investments in skills development and greater efforts by companies to upskill their workforce to perform new and higher order roles in complementarity with machines.

Adoption of 4IR technologies can increase efficiency and productivity. They enable real-time tracking of supply chains for production and inventory management of raw materials and finished goods. Use of artificial intelligence and machine learning can provide insights into consumer behavior to customize production. Robotic process automation can relieve tedious and repetitive labor-intensive activities, allowing time for higher order functions. Augmented reality and virtual reality can be helpful to train workers in new tasks that they were not familiar with, or skilled in, earlier. Application of 4IR technologies helps developing countries move up the value chain in their products and services. Timely skills development can ensure that automation and artificial intelligence can benefit workers at large.

The study has resulted in a suite of country reports for Cambodia, Indonesia, the Philippines, and Viet Nam, and a synthesis report that captures common elements across the four. They seek to provide policy makers with research and evidence-based solutions for skills and talent development to strengthen the countries' readiness for a transition to 4IR.

The role of governments is crucial in ensuring equitable access to skills development. We expect to see a new balance between physical and virtual workplaces as the gig economy, where employers increasingly rely on part-time freelance workers on short-term contracts, takes firmer position, and widespread digital transformation of citizen services that call for basic digital capabilities in all population groups and rising opportunities for those with advanced digital skills. Job losses will be real, however, a well-prepared 4IR strategy with industry transformation road maps that are recommended in the study can convert disruptions to opportunities to pivot the workforce to new and modern occupations.

The study was completed prior to the coronavirus disease (COVID-19). It is apparent that COVID-19 is accelerating digital transformation. Companies deploying 4IR technologies are likely to recover faster from heavy disruptions arising from the pandemic and be more resilient in the future. Beyond COVID-19, market analysts predict a 'new normal' where digital strategies adopted during the lockdown due to the pandemic will pick up pace. Consumer and producer behavior will most likely be altered permanently with greater digital exposure. The study's recommendations to strengthen widespread digital capabilities, enhance online/distance learning, digital platforms, education technology (EdTech), and simulation-based learning have become more relevant in the aftermath of COVID-19. The study also points to the scope for closer collaboration between public and private sectors, which is also quite relevant in the COVID-19 context. The findings of this study are thus very timely in the discourse to facilitate a sustainable recovery from COVID-19, as countries aspire for accelerating economic diversification and boosting competitiveness using the pandemic as an opportunity for structural reforms.

We welcome your feedback on this report and continued engagement with all stakeholders.

Woochong Um
Director General
Sustainable Development and
Climate Change Department

Ramesh Subramaniam
Director General
South East Asia Department

Preface and Acknowledgments

The ADB study *Reaping the Benefits of Industry 4.0 Through Skills Development in High-Growth Industries in Southeast Asia* marks our effort to bridge research, policy, and practice on the implications of the Fourth Industrial Revolution (4IR) on future job markets. To effectively address this forward-looking topic, the study made use of various sources of secondary information and sought to triangulate information from different primary sources. It included a survey of employers, a survey of training institutions on their readiness for 4IR, and analysis of data from online job portals from each country to assess trends in skills demand. The study used a modeling exercise to estimate job displacement and gains in the selected industries in each of the countries. A review of the policy landscape based on benchmarks from international trends and experiences provides the basis for the action points that countries can use to harness the potential of Industry 4.0 to increase productivity, facilitate skills development, and incentivize industry.

The findings and recommendations from the study point us to collaborate with our partners to implement decisive changes in renewing skills development strategies that acquire a full life cycle approach to skills development. This means that there are no degrees or certificates for life and constant renewals and upskilling are essential. The preponderant focus on institution-based training needs to give way to more flexible and multimodal training to include bootcamps, e-learning, and work-place based training. Training for digital skills at basic, intermediate, and higher levels needs a significant ramp up as workplaces undergo digital transformation.

As co-team leaders, we thank the consultant team led by Fraser Thompson, director, AlphaBeta, for an excellent partnership in this study. The core team in AlphaBeta include Konstantin Matthies, engagement manager; Genevieve Lim, engagement manager; and Richard McClellan, senior advisor. We thank AlphaBeta's national experts Ananto Kusuma Seta (Indonesia), Dao Quang Vinh (Viet Nam), Jose Roland A. Moya (Philippines), and Trevor Sworn (Cambodia). AlphaBeta's team developed the analytical model for the study and collaborated closely with ADB's team to bring new insights and directions and we are grateful for this professional collaboration.

Brajesh Panth, Ayako Inagaki, Robert Guild, and Rana Hasan provided valuable guidance to the study. We thank Shamit Chakravarti, Lynette Perez, Yumiko Yamakawa, and Sakiko Tanaka in ADB's Southeast Asia Human and Social Development Division and Paul Vandenberg and Elisabetta Gentile from the Economic Research and Regional Cooperation Department for providing inputs at various stages of the study and Sophea Mar, Sutarum Wiryono, Vinh Ngo from ADB resident missions in Cambodia, Indonesia, and Viet Nam, respectively, for their valuable support and country-level consultations. Iris Miranda, Sheela Rances, and Dorothy Geronimo from ADB, and Jannis Hoh, Shivin Kohli, and Anna Lim from AlphaBeta provided timely coordination of meetings and activities during the study. We thank April Gallega for coordinating the editing of the reports for publication and Mike Cortes for the cover designs.

The study would not have been possible if not for the leadership of senior government and industry representatives and senior members of the academia in the respective countries. We were heartened to note the high level of interest on the topic of 4IR. In each of the countries, there are already several important initiatives underway to enable industry and companies to move toward application of 4IR. The study was closely coordinated with senior government and industry participants, specifically on the selection of the two sectors for detailed study for each of the countries. The emerging findings of the study were shared in country level workshops. Senior officials and key counterparts consulted are listed at the end of each country report.

We look forward to discussions in taking forward the study's policy recommendations.

Shanti Jagannathan
Principal Education Specialist
Sustainable Development
and Climate Change Department

Sameer Khatiwada
Social Sector Specialist
South East Asia Department

Abbreviations

4IR	Industry 4.0 or Fourth Industrial Revolution
ADB	Asian Development Bank
AI	artificial intelligence
ASEAN	Association of Southeast Asian Nations
BLK	*Balai Latihan Kerja* (vocational training center)
CMEA	Coordinating Ministry of Economic Affairs
CMHDCA	Coordinating Ministry of Human Development and Cultural Affairs
F&B	food and beverage
GDP	gross domestic product
IFLS	Indonesian Family Life Survey
ILO	International Labour Organization
IoT	Internet of Things
MENC	Ministry of Education and Culture
MSMEs	micro, small, and medium-sized enterprises
MOI	Ministry of Industry
MOM	Ministry of Manpower
MORT	Ministry of Research and Technology
STEP	Systematic Tracking of Exchanges in Procurement
TVET	technical and vocational education and training
UNESCO	United Nations Educational, Scientific and Cultural Organization

Executive Summary

Background of the Study

The future of jobs is at the heart of the development conundrum for developing countries in the Asia and Pacific region in the coming years, and preparing the workforce of the future with the right skills and capabilities is central to the technical and vocational education and training (TVET) and skills development portfolio of the Asian Development Bank (ADB). In recent years, the influence of disruptive technologies on jobs and labor markets has intensified worries around extensive job losses arising from automation and potential disappearance of the comparative advantage of countries based on competitive labor costs. Hence, the capacity of developing countries to effectively address the transition to Industry 4.0 or the Fourth Industrial Revolution (4IR) has become an area of concern. To better understand the implications of 4IR on the future of jobs and to assess the readiness of education and training institutions to prepare for future labor markets, ADB undertook a study that seeks to capture anticipated transformations on jobs, tasks, and skills and to outline policy directions to prepare the workforce for future jobs.

Scope of the Study

The study covered Cambodia, Indonesia, the Philippines, and Viet Nam, and included the following features:

(i)   It focused on two industries in each country deemed important for growth, employment, and 4IR: tourism and garments in Cambodia, food and beverage (F&B) manufacturing and automotive manufacturing in Indonesia, information technology and business process outsourcing (IT-BPO) and electronics in the Philippines, and agro-processing and logistics in Viet Nam. The table shows the economic importance of each industry in each economy.

(ii)   The study includes a survey of employers in the chosen industries, a modeling exercise to estimate job displacement and gains, a survey of training institutions on their readiness for 4IR, and analysis of data from online job portals from each country to assess trends in skills demand.

(iii)   The policy landscape was assessed, based on benchmarks derived from international trends and experiences, for its ability to harness the potential of 4IR to increase productivity, facilitate skills development, and incentivize industry.

(iv)   Recommendations suggest how to strengthen policy approaches to 4IR, especially the investments needed for skills and training, new approaches to deliver them, and strategies and actions to enhance the readiness of each country's workforce for 4IR.

The COVID-19 Effect

The study was undertaken and completed prior to the spread of the coronavirus disease (COVID-19), which has caused unprecedented disruptions to labor markets and to the activities of the workforce across the world. This study's policy recommendations and strategies to strengthen widespread digital capabilities, enhance online and/or distance learning, digital platforms, education technology, and simulation-based learning have become all the more relevant in the aftermath of COVID-19. The key approaches discussed and elaborated in the report bear great relevance to the current context of countries experiencing nationwide closures of schools and training institutes. The expectation is also that post-COVID-19, there will be operating procedures in the workplace that constitute a "new normal" and will require enhanced digital capabilities. Hence, the findings of this study and the follow-on policy directions are timely and crucial for facilitating a sustainable COVID-19 recovery strategy.

The two sectors chosen for the study in Indonesia—food and beverage (F&B) and auto sectors—have been adversely affected by the pandemic. In F&B, the expectation is that there would be lasting shifts in consumer behavior in dealing with the COVID-19 response. Food retailers are likely to scale up e-commerce. The logistics part of the sector in storing, transporting, and delivering is likely to become more tech-oriented, calling for new skills and talent. Similarly, in the auto industry, recovery after COVID-19 will entail embracing digital supply chains and launching digital sales and marketing initiatives. Hence the upskilling and reskilling on 4IR-related occupations is even more urgent for the revival of the economy and economic stimulus needed post-COVID-19.

The study obviously does not address the implications of COVID-19 in Indonesia. However, the policy directions and future investments for higher order skills, particularly in the digital domain are eminently suitable for the country to reimagine new beginnings for the two sectors.

Key Findings for Indonesia

The F&B and automotive manufacturing industries were selected for an analysis of the implications of 4IR for jobs, tasks, and skills in Indonesia. These industries are important for national employment, growth, international competitiveness, and relevance for 4IR technologies. The F&B manufacturing industry accounts for 4% of total employment, 6.6% of gross domestic product (GDP), and 4.1% of total exports. Although the automotive manufacturing industry only accounts for 0.13% of total employment, it contributes to 2% of GDP (proxied by the transportation equipment industry) and 4% of total exports in the country, and has significant opportunities to go up the value chain, particularly with the adoption of 4IR technologies. These two industries are also included in the Government of Indonesia's list of five priority industries for 4IR (the other three industries are textiles, chemicals, and electronics).

The study finds that 4IR will have a transformational effect on jobs and skills in the F&B and automotive manufacturing industries with great potential for positive gains in jobs and productivity—which can be reaped through adequate investments in skills and training. Key findings from the study include:

(i) **4IR will bring positive net job gains in the food and beverage and automotive sectors.**

    (a) Application of 4IR technologies will lead to a loss of jobs arising from automation; however, it could also lead to new labor demand through productivity increases, and the study estimates a positive net effect on jobs in both industries. While 26% of the current workforce in the F&B industry and 29% in the automotive manufacturing industry could potentially be displaced by 4IR technologies, there will also be additional demand. It is estimated that there will be 41% additional labor demand in the F&B industry and 30% in the automotive manufacturing industry, leading to positive job gains.

    (b) Significant productivity improvements are expected in the F&B and automotive manufacturing industries with the application of 4IR technologies. The study reports that 52% of employers in the F&B industry and 76% in the automotive manufacturing industry expect productivity improvements of over 25% from the application of 4IR technologies by 2030. More than a third of employers in the F&B manufacturing industry and 46% of employers in the automotive manufacturing industry anticipate over 50% increase in productivity through 4IR by 2025. However, it is also acknowledged that the cost of adopting 4IR technology is high.

    (c) The adoption of 4IR technologies is already underway with 41% of employers in the F&B manufacturing industry reported that they were already adopting 4IR technologies in their operations and 56% stating they would do so by 2025. In the automotive manufacturing industry, 48% of employers reported that they were already adopting 4IR technologies, with 60% stating that they would do so by 2025.

    (d) The study warns that there are no guarantees that displaced workers can seamlessly move into new jobs that will emerge from productivity increases, without adequate and timely investments in skills development. There will be a need to update training for changing task and skill profiles in the transition to a 4IR workplace.

(ii) **4IR calls for higher order tasks with an expected decline of physical tasks.**

    (a) The study finds that the importance of routine physical tasks will decline with the application of 4IR, and analytical and nonroutine tasks will become more prominent. In the F&B manufacturing industry, by 2030, workers could spend an additional 13.5% of time in a working week on analytical and nonroutine interpersonal tasks, with over 13% of time reduced from physical tasks. The automotive manufacturing industry will see nearly a 10% increase in analytical and nonroutine interpersonal tasks, while there is an expected reduction of about 10% in all physical tasks (routine and nonroutine). This is consistent with the growing use of robotics in automotive assembly lines and 4IR technologies in F&B manufacturing.

    (b) With the diminishing manual and physical activities in a 4IR workplace, skills such as judgment and decision-making and critical thinking are expected to become far more important in both industries by 2030 as a result of 4IR. Employers surveyed as well as information from online job portals illustrate the growing importance of such skills compared to routine physical and just technical skills. In the F&B manufacturing industry, employees need to move from basic skills to intermediate skill levels. In the automotive manufacturing industry, skilling up may be required and most workers will require basic digital skills, going beyond basic computer literacy.

(iii) **Alleviating skills shortages and augmenting skill levels in both industries is crucial for 4IR.**

    (a) While preparing the workforce for 4IR, it is important to address the overall skills shortages and a lack of preparation of people for the workplace. Nearly a third of employers in the F&B manufacturing industry and 44% of automotive manufacturing industry employers reported that graduates hired in the past year were not adequately prepared by their pre-hire education and/or training.

    (b) In the F&B industry, 46% of employers and 78% in the automotive manufacturing industry reported large variations in the quality of vocational secondary graduates depending on region and education provider. The industry's endorsement of credentials will become even more important for the employability of graduates.

    (c) Employers in both industries stress the importance of training and skills development in preparation for 4IR. On-the-job training will be crucial to deliver the required skill shift. The F&B industry will require "one-person training" (the training of one worker in one skill from the average level required by their occupation in their industry in 2018 to the required level in 2030) of an additional 51.2 million people and the automotive manufacturing industry of 1 million additional people. In both industries, on-the-job training will be a critical form of skills development that needs to be expanded. Education and training institutions need to step up the preparation of graduates for entry-level positions.

(iv) **While training institutions report strong engagement with industry, there is a significant mismatch in perceptions on graduate preparedness at the entry level.**

    (a) Encouragingly, most training institutions surveyed reported a high level of engagement with businesses and frequent updates of curriculum. Regular curriculum reviews are particularly crucial to keep pace with the skill changes related to 4IR. Of the training institutions surveyed, 72% review and update their curricula annually. Engagement with business also appears to be strong with 45% of training institutions stating they communicate and coordinate with employers in relevant industries several times a year. Of the training institutions surveyed, 84% reported working with employers on train-the-teacher programs to improve industry relevance. Over three-quarters of institutions reported they organize apprenticeships or gather inputs for curriculum from industry. However, the study suggests there is a need to evaluate the quality of industry partnerships and to systematically address the 4IR skills needed.

    (b) Despite the reported close engagement with industry, the study finds a significant mismatch in the perceptions on skill preparation between employers and training institutions. While 96% of training institutions believe their graduates are well-prepared for the 4IR workforce, only 33% of employers in the F&B industry and 30% in the automotive manufacturing industry agree.

    (c) Of the training institutions surveyed, 68% reported they already have dedicated programs related to 4IR skills, while 90% reported plans to develop or expand programs for 4IR by 2025. While this is an encouraging trend, it is critical to assess the quality and relevance of such training and their alignment with employer needs. A structured needs assessment for training for 4IR is needed as 90% of training institutions surveyed said additional financial and technical support is needed for 4IR skills development.

(v) **Training delivery needs to embrace 4IR technologies and approaches.**

    (a) The study found promising trends in training institutions of adopting technology for teaching and learning, particularly digital skills programs. Over half the training institutions surveyed are reportedly running digital programs for improving digital literacy. Nearly 70%

of institutions are using online self-learning tools. However, the deployment of advanced technologies for transforming traditional training approaches is still limited—only 19% of training institutions adopted virtual learning platforms and only 16% are using virtual and/or augmented reality in training. Moreover, the quality and standards used in digital literacy are yet to be ascertained.

(b) Training institutions have a strong focus on instructor and teacher performance assessment. However, exposure of teachers and trainers to adopting new delivery methods appears limited. Over 80% of training institutions surveyed have annual or semiannual performance reviews for teachers, and only 55% of institutions provide for teachers to have on-the-job time devoted to gaining practical knowledge and new teaching techniques.

(vi) **Indonesia's 4IR policies and strategies are in the right direction and need active implementation.**

(a) The strategy Making Indonesia 4.0 has a clearly articulated vision and is robustly backed by local data as well as studies on international trends in 4IR technology adoption and productivity benefits. The Coordinating Ministry of Economic Affairs' plans to envision a unified skills development strategy across ministries is a step in the right direction.

(b) Greater efforts are needed to promote inclusiveness linked to 4IR. There is limited evidence of strong government focus to enable underserved groups access to opportunities to train in preparation for 4IR. There is also a need to consider updating social protection mechanisms for regular workers as well as for the expected surge of on-demand or flexible workers, which is expected to rapidly rise in Indonesia and globally.

(c) There is currently a lack of flexible education pathways linked to 4IR. The country still has a strong emphasis on traditional qualifications attained through the education system or competency assessments, as opposed to past work experiences and the skills gained through them. Given the fast-changing terrain in technology, more agile and on-demand skills development modules and opportunities need to be created.

Key Recommendations

The study, drawing on the findings of employer survey and training institution survey together with an assessment of policy, identifies seven recommendations for Indonesia to strengthen its preparedness toward 4IR. A multi-stakeholder approach to the actions in each of these recommendations will be critical to their effectiveness. For each of them, a potential lead (from either the government or private sector) has been identified, alongside a list of stakeholders suggested to be engaged when developing and implementing the recommended actions. These recommended actions include:

(i) **Develop 4IR transformation road maps for key sectors.** The Government of Indonesia could strengthen coordination mechanisms among government departments on 4IR and consider preparing industry transformation road maps to better integrate the 4IR strategy with the country's overarching economic priorities. Singapore's Industry Transformation Maps, which provide information on technology impacts, career pathways, skills required for different occupations, and reskilling options for different industries is an example. Industry-specific road maps for the F&B and automotive manufacturing industries (with the other three industries the Government of Indonesia identified as important for 4IR) could be a useful starting point to strengthen competitiveness in the era of 4IR.

(ii) **Develop a series of industry-led TVET programs targeting skills for 4IR.** Indonesia has ongoing efforts to improve linkages between TVET and industry, which can be built upon to develop a series of industry-led TVET programs specifically for 4IR in priority sectors encompassing new flexible courses, credentials, and industry recognition mechanisms. The initial focus could be on the F&B and automotive manufacturing industries (and the remaining three priority industries for 4IR). The McKinsey-founded independent nonprofit Generation is a good example of an industry-led program. Over 30,000 people from 13 countries have graduated from its programs. Of this number, 81% were employed within 3 months after graduation and received salaries two to six times higher than their previous earnings.

(iii) **Strengthen quality assurance mechanisms for training institutions.** With several training institutions already undertaking courses for 4IR, it is recommended to revisit quality assurance mechanisms, particularly to address the quality of training of trainers programs and industry partnerships and to consider mechanisms to strengthen them. The study suggests that industry benchmarks and standards are crucial to develop new curricular domains for 4IR that can be used by training institutions.

(iv) **Upgrade training delivery through 4IR technology in classrooms and improved training facilities.** Technology adoption in the classroom in Indonesia for the world of 4IR appears limited. Greater deployment of new technologies, such as virtual reality, augmented reality, and simulation would help to strengthen workforce readiness. Given the substantial need for on-the-job training for reskilling and upskilling, it is recommended to explore potential digital platforms for delivery of skills development at scale. This is in line with government's priority for online education. These new approaches need to permeate high schools, TVET institutions, polytechnics, and higher education institutions. Preparation of a systematic suite of 4IR methodologies for use in training delivery would be valuable.

(v) **Develop flexible and modular skill certification programs.** It is recommended that Indonesia explore the development of flexible skill certification programs that recognize skills attainment outside traditional education channels. A good example of a skill-based accreditation system is the Malaysian Skills Certification Program, under which skill certificates are granted to workers who do not have formal educational qualifications, but who have obtained relevant knowledge, experience, and skills in the workplace to enhance their career prospects. Given the large-scale requirements for reskilling and upskilling, industry-led certification for gradual progression in skills through modular programs for possible stacking of credentials is required.

(vi) **Implement an incentive scheme for firms to train employees for 4IR.** Despite the substantial productivity gains 4IR technologies could bring about, employer training rates remain low due to a number of market failures relating to information asymmetries around the benefits of training, as well as weak incentives for employers. It is thus critical to develop a set of support programs to encourage firms to invest in relevant 4IR training for their workers. An important area would be to prepare guidelines and operationalize the government's tax incentive scheme for firms to invest in skills development. The study finds that on-the-job training will become even more crucial to cope with job displacements and to prepare workers for new occupations. Large-scale efforts for reskilling and upskilling with industry partnerships will be needed for a successful transition to a 4IR workplace.

(vii) **Formulate new approaches and measures to strengthen inclusion and social protection in the context of 4IR.** It is critical to ensure the country's journey toward 4IR is inclusive in providing opportunities for the underprivileged. Support for training for three types of workers is needed: entry-level workers, workers at risk of job displacement, and workers needing upskilling.

Modern delivery mechanisms, including digital platforms with industry-recognized credentials, can be the means to reach the underprivileged in remote locations. It is recommended that cost–benefit analyses of several policy options for the social protection of on-demand or flexible workers be conducted and promising schemes piloted to test their broader applicability. These could include exploring policy approaches to enhance the income security for on-demand workers (e.g., in Australia, workers on short-term contracts are entitled to an increment of 25% each hour worked compared to a worker doing the same job on an ongoing basis), or working with key employers to champion corporate policies mandating income stability for on-demand workers.

While these recommendations apply to both the F&B and automotive manufacturing industries, a set of priorities unique to each industry should be considered when implementing the respective actions. These include:

(i) **Food and beverage manufacturing industry.** Improve the quality of industry-relevant education and training courses to ensure stronger alignment with the skills demanded by employers; address the relative lack of private-sector support for 4IR adoption and skills training; and prioritize 4IR technologies and skillsets that could address large postharvest losses.

(ii) **Automotive manufacturing industry.** Prioritize 4IR adoption and related skills development efforts for MSMEs; support 4IR knowledge transfer from large multinational companies to MSMEs; and foster stronger coordination between *Balai Latihan Kerja* and individual company-led training institutes.

CHAPTER 1

The Industry 4.0 Skills Challenge

This chapter investigates the demand and supply of skills driven by Industry 4.0 or the Fourth Industrial Revolution (4IR) technology adoption for both the food and beverage (F&B) and automotive manufacturing industries in Indonesia. The analysis used a range of data, including employer surveys and interviews, online job board data, and national labor market statistics.

In both industries, the impact of 4IR will be transformative for jobs and skills. The analysis shows that despite widespread concerns of significant automation and loss of jobs associated with 4IR, the net impact on jobs for both industries to 2030 is likely to be positive, with more jobs being created than displaced. However, there are no guarantees that displaced workers can seamlessly move into these new jobs without investment in skills development. In the current workforce, 26% in the F&B industry and 29% in the automotive manufacturing industry could potentially be displaced by 4IR technologies. While the overall patterns of impact in the two industries are similar, there are some important differences. For example, in the automotive manufacturing industry, the net effect on jobs very marginal, only 1% larger than the displacement impact. Also, while displacement in the automotive manufacturing industry almost entirely affects manual workers, the F&B processing industries are likely to see significant displacement among customer-facing (approximately 29,000 workers) and administrative workers (approximately 11,000 workers).

In terms of skills, judgment and decision-making and critical thinking skills will become more important by 2030 in both industries. In the F&B manufacturing industry, workers need to move from basic skills to an intermediate skill level. In the automotive manufacturing industry, most workers will need basic digital skills, going beyond basic computer literacy.

It is estimated the F&B manufacturing industry will demand close to 51.2 million and the automotive manufacturing industry 1.0 million additional person trainings by 2030.[1] In both industries, on-the-job training will be the critical form of skills development, combined with enhanced training opportunities within formal institutions and through digital platforms.

Industry 4.0 and the Relevance for Indonesia

4IR is a widely used term to refer to a range of new technologies impacting the workplace. The term was first conceptualized to describe data exchange technologies used in manufacturing. However, it has now acquired a broader meaning to refer to technologies applied across all industries, including services

---

[1] One-person training refers to training one worker, in one skill from the average level required by their occupation in their industry in 2018 to the required level in 2030.

industries.[2] These technologies include, among others, cyberphysical systems, the Internet of Things (IoT), artificial intelligence, cloud computing, and cognitive computing.

4IR is a different concept from previous industrial revolutions, both in scope and technologies (Figure 1). The first industrial revolution in the 18th century was marked by a transition from hand production methods to machines through the use of steam power and waterpower. The second industrial revolution in the 19th century involved the use of extensive railroad networks and the telegraph to allow faster transfer of people and ideas, combined with factory electrification and the creation of mass production assembly line approaches. The third industrial revolution occurred in the late 20th century and is often referred to as the digital revolution, involving the use of computers, the internet, robots and automation, and electronics. 4IR builds on these past industrial revolutions, but includes a far broader array of technologies with applicability across all industries. In this regard, it is fundamentally different from the past industrial revolutions in its potential implications for economies and the workforce.

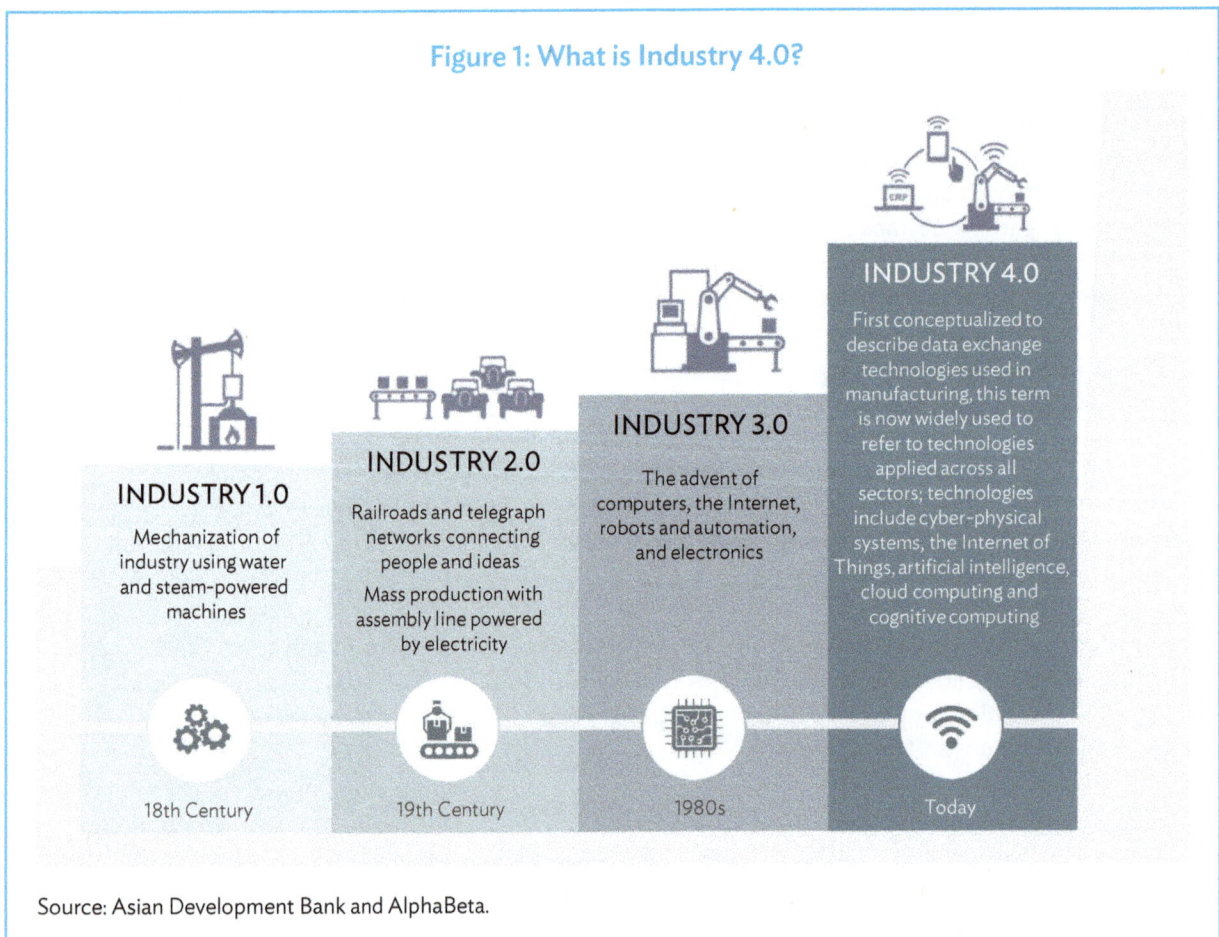

Figure 1: What is Industry 4.0?

INDUSTRY 1.0
Mechanization of industry using water and steam-powered machines

18th Century

INDUSTRY 2.0
Railroads and telegraph networks connecting people and ideas

Mass production with assembly line powered by electricity

19th Century

INDUSTRY 3.0
The advent of computers, the Internet, robots and automation, and electronics

1980s

INDUSTRY 4.0
First conceptualized to describe data exchange technologies used in manufacturing, this term is now widely used to refer to technologies applied across all sectors; technologies include cyber-physical systems, the Internet of Things, artificial intelligence, cloud computing and cognitive computing

Today

Source: Asian Development Bank and AlphaBeta.

2   K. Schwab. 2017. *The Fourth Industrial Revolution.* New York: Currency. https://books.google.com.sg/books?hl=en&lr=&id=ST_FD AAAQBAJ&oi=fnd&pg=PR7&dq=klaus+schwab+fourth+industrial+revolution&ots=DTnvbTqvTQ&sig=aOLqcUCFsLKbNpj Wa5kr2Sjzhu4#v=onepage&q=klaus%20schwab%20fourth%20industrial%20revolution&f=false.

What could 4IR mean for Indonesia? Much of the past literature demonstrates the potential productivity impact could be significant. A study by McKinsey & Company in 2018, for example, showed that early 4IR adopters in the Association of Southeast Asian Nations (ASEAN) demonstrated high productivity gains of 10% to 50%.[3]

With the large potential impact of 4IR technology adoption, there are concerns about the impact on employment. Most concerns revolve around fears that 4IR could lead to mass unemployment as (i) workers are replaced by machines; or (ii) workers do not have the right skills to effectively work alongside 4IR technologies, or transition into new emerging jobs.

Understanding how the skills landscape is likely to change under 4IR is difficult, given the rapid pace of technology. This means traditional approaches of assessing skill gaps, often relying on time-intensive processes to collect data, which quickly become outdated, may no longer be suitable. This study explores a new approach to understanding the labor market implications of 4IR that tries to address gaps in previous studies. Some of the key design features of the study include:

(i) **Use of local data.** The study uses a variety of local data sources, including the RAND Indonesian Family Life Survey (IFLS),[4] job portal data,[5] as well as surveys[6] of Indonesian businesses in the F&B and automotive manufacturing industries.

(ii) **Use of current market information.** Given the rapid change in the labor market, existing labor market surveys can become quickly obsolete. To address this concern, this report uses information on skill profiles for current occupations advertised in online job portals in Indonesia.

(iii) **Focus on supply, not just demand.** Much of past research examined changes in occupations and skills related to 4IR.[7] This study goes further by examining the supply landscape, including understanding the volume and types of training required (e.g., on-the-job training, short professional courses, and others). For this study, a survey of training institutions in Indonesia was undertaken to understand the degree to which they are currently addressing the shifts in demand for skills for 4IR.[8]

---

[3]   Arbulu, I. et al. 2018. *Industry 4.0: Reinvigorating ASEAN Manufacturing for the Future.* McKinsey & Company. 8 February. https://www. mckinsey.com/business-functions/operations/our-insights/industry-4-0-reinvigorating-asean-manufacturing-for-the-future.

[4]   The IFLS is an ongoing longitudinal survey in Indonesia. The sample is representative of about 83% of the Indonesian population and contains over 30,000 individuals living in 13 of the 27 provinces in the country. The IFLS includes a questionnaire of tasks and skills used by respondents for their respective occupations. This data was used to understand current skill and task profiles by occupation and industry.

[5]   The study analyzed over 180 job profiles across the F&B and automotive manufacturing industries, scraped from the job portal Karir for the type and level of skills required for the job. This data was used to (i) give an accurate picture of skill demand today, and (ii) predict the trends in skill requirement changes as compared to historic data.

[6]   Overall, more than 117 Indonesian businesses were surveyed. Not all respondents completed the entire survey questionnaire. Therefore, the sample size used in each of the analyses differed and the relevant number of observations are stated in each case.

[7]   A thorough review of the relevant literature can be found in Asian Development Bank (ADB). 2018. *Asian Development Outlook 2018 – How Technology Affects Jobs.* https://www.adb.org/publications/asian-development-outlook-2018-how-technology-affects-jobs.

[8]   The study included a survey of 44 training institutions in Indonesia.

Industry Selection

Two industries were chosen to conduct this analysis of 4IR implications for the demand and supply of skills. A two-step methodology was used to select the industries:

(i) **Shortlisting industries prioritized by the Government of Indonesia for future growth or for 4IR application.** This included reviewing the 2015–2035 National Industrial Development Master Plan and the Making Industry 4.0 strategy.

(ii) **Scoring and ranking shortlisted industries according to a set of criteria:**
   (a) How significant is the industry's contribution to the country's employment?
   (b) Does it exhibit strong recent employment growth?
   (c) Are its exports internationally competitive?
   (d) Is 4IR of relevance to the industry?
   (e) Is the relevant data available for the industry analysis?

The industries were then tested with various stakeholders during a country consultation conducted in July 2019. Based on this process, the F&B and automotive manufacturing industries were selected for the analysis:

(i) **Food and beverage manufacturing.** This industry is a major contributor to Indonesia's total employment, accounting for over 4.5 million workers, and almost 4% of total employment in 2015, according to latest available data from Badan Pusat Statistik (Statistics Indonesia, BPS). This is over a quarter of employment across all processing industries. Industry employment has also been growing rapidly at over 10% in 2013–2015. As a result, the industry is a major source of economic activity, contributing 6.6% to gross domestic product (GDP) in 2018. The annual contribution to GDP has been growing by 8.5% year-on-year since 2015. The industry is a key priority in Indonesia's 2015–2035 National Industrial Development Master Plan and more importantly for this study, one of the five priority industries under Making Indonesia 4.0, Indonesia's Industry 4.0 development strategy. During country consultations with various ministries and industry associations, a strong push emerged to further grow this industry for greater export competitiveness. In particular, stakeholders articulated the ambition for Indonesia to be the ASEAN F&B powerhouse by 2030. 4IR could be a key driver to achieving this as productivity gains are potentially high.

(ii) **Automotive manufacturing.** Similar to the F&B manufacturing industry, the automotive manufacturing industry is one of the five priority industries under Making Indonesia 4.0. The broader manufacturing of transport equipment is a key priority in Indonesia's 2015–2035 National Industrial Development Master Plan. Both government and industry stakeholders that engaged in country consultations shared a desire to move up the value chain and expand into new products, such as being able to produce electric vehicles by 2030. While significantly smaller than in the F&B manufacturing industry, employment in the automotive manufacturing industry is also growing at rapid pace of 7.6% annually from 2013 to 2015, according to the latest publicly available data from BPS. The transportation equipment industry contributed almost 2% to GDP in 2018, growing at 4.1% annually since 2015, and accounted for close to 4% of exports in 2017 according to the World Bank. Micro, small, and medium-sized enterprises (MSMEs) play a major role in this industry—70% of enterprises in the automotive manufacturing industry are MSMEs focused on supplying parts to large manufacturers. Stakeholders described potential blind spots of unmet skilling needs in such small parts manufacturing.

Food and Beverage Manufacturing Industry

The F&B manufacturing industry could be transformed by 4IR. The study estimates that 4IR technologies could displace 26% of today's employment in the industry, close to 1.4 million workers. This is based on the industry breakdown of tasks currently performed by workers and how employers expect those tasks to change given the adoption of 4IR technologies (based on the employer survey). Clearly, there is a great deal of uncertainty with some of these future projections, however, contrary to some perceptions that 4IR will lead to mass unemployment, the research provides an overall optimistic assessment. Net employment from 4IR may actually rise in the F&B manufacturing industry as displacement effects from 4IR are offset by employment linked to productivity gains, i.e., the income effect. However, the skills required by workers in this industry will need to change markedly, with the demand for evaluation, judgment, and decision-making, and critical thinking expected to increase significantly. Much of this skills development needs to come from on-the-job training and, in sum, there needs to be 51.2 million additional person training (footnote 1) by 2030. However, given a third of employers in the F&B manufacturing industry surveyed said fresh graduates are inadequately prepared by their pre-hire education and/or training institutions, there is also a need for transformation in formal and professional training and education, and a need to explore new delivery mechanisms on scale such as digital platforms.

Relevance of Industry 4.0

Industry 4.0 represents a large opportunity for the F&B industry. The use of big data and IoT can enhance demand forecasting and production planning to improve customer service levels, thus boosting profit margins. On the cost side of the equation, analyzing detailed, real-time data on everything from suppliers' inventory and shipments in transit, to downstream customer demand, allows manufacturing companies to tighten inventory control and maximize production capacity.[9]

There are various Industry 4.0 technologies of relevance for the F&B industry, ranging from digital technologies enabling smart factories through to IoT to improve supply chain monitoring. This is particularly important for Indonesia's context, where industry stakeholders have cited postharvest losses of as high as 15 % of the original harvest volume every year.[10] McKinsey & Company estimated that productivity could increase by up to 50% through adopting relevant technologies in the F&B industry in ASEAN (footnote 6).

Some key technologies include:

(i)   **Internet of Things.** IoT refers to networks of sensors and actuators embedded in machines and other physical objects that connect with one another and the internet. It has a wide range of applications, including data collection, monitoring, decision-making, and process optimization (footnote 13). Radio frequency identification tags on containers can track products as they move from the factory to stores, allowing companies to avoid stock-outs and losses. Singapore's YCH Group reduced stock turnaround time by 20% in a 220,000-square foot warehouse of

---

[9]   J. Woetzl et al. 2014. *Southeast Asia at the Crossroads: Three Paths to Prosperity.* McKinsey Global Institute. November. https://www.mckinsey.com/~/media/McKinsey/Featured%20Insights/Asia%20Pacific/Three%20paths%20to%20sustained%20economic%20growth%20in%20Southeast%20Asia/MGI%20SE%20Asia_Executive%20summary_November%202014.ashx.

[10] Based on consultation with KADIN in July 2019.

close to 3,000 stock-keeping units by using radio frequency identification systems for more accurate pallet sorting.[11]

(ii) **Artificial intelligence and big data.** Big data refers to the ability to analyze extremely large volumes of data, extract insights, and act on them closer to real time. This has a range of benefits in the F&B industry, including being able to use predictive analytics to fine-tune production volumes and processes, better supply chain management, and greater insights on customer segments.

(iii) **Industry robotics.** Industrial robots can significantly improve productivity in the F&B industry and there has been increased investment in robots in this industry in response to drivers such as wage costs, 24 x 7 production requirements, and high levels of staff turnover. Robots are increasingly used for functions ranging from forklift operations through to bottling operations. The food, beverage, and personal care industry is estimated to account for 13% of all industrial robot sales in the Americas.[12]

(iv) **Additive manufacturing.** This describes the technologies that build three-dimension (3D) objects by adding layer-upon-layer of material. Additive manufacturing is still nascent in the food industry, but is receiving increasing interest. Benefits include product differentiation, product customization, and direct-to-consumer relationships. For example, it could lead to the creation of unique food formulations for dietary needs, simplified distribution into hard-to-reach locations, and customized medical and nutritional supplements.[13]

Adoption and understanding of 4IR technologies across the F&B manufacturing industry in Indonesia is somewhat mixed (Figure 2). Of companies surveyed, 41% agreed or strongly agreed when asked whether they adopted 4IR technologies in their operations and 59% claimed to have a good understanding of what 4IR technologies were of relevance to their industry. Cost remains a critical barrier to adoption: 45% of employers said the cost of technology is a significant barrier for their company to adopt 4IR in alignment with research by the International Labour Organization (ILO).

Of the employers in the F&B manufacturing industry surveyed in Indonesia, 73% anticipated productivity improvements of between 10%–100% from adopting 4IR over the next 5 years (Figure 3).

Skills Demand Analysis

Employment Implications

The analysis examines two factors influencing employment in the F&B manufacturing industry related to 4IR:

(i) **Displacement effect.** This refers to the number of jobs lost due to the automation of tasks automatable through the application of 4IR technology. Displacement of jobs occurs only if the tasks automated by technology make up such a significant proportion of the workers' time spent at work or are so essential to his or her role that the worker is no longer needed. The analysis estimates this displacement at 26% of today's employment or close to 1.4 million workers.

---

[11]   Intermec. 2010. YCH Group Selects Intermec Fixed Vehicle Computer to Improve Supply Chain Management. https://www.varinsights.com/doc/ych-group-selects-intermec-fixed-vehicle-0004.

[12]   R. Sullivan. 2019. Increased Role of Robots in Food Manufacturing. *Food Quality & Safety*. 25 February. https://www.foodqualityandsafety.com/article/increased-role-of-robots-in-food-manufacturing/.

[13]   Deloitte. 2015. *3D Opportunity Serves it up: Additive Manufacturing and Food.* https://www2.deloitte.com/us/en/insights/focus/3d-opportunity/3d-printing-in-the-food-industry.html.

Figure 2: Food and Beverage Employer Sentiment Toward 4IR in Indonesia

F&B: 4IR readiness

Companies in the F&B industry claim to have some understanding of Industry 4.0 and plan to adopt it going forward.

Respondents (%)

Legend: Don't know | Disagree | Agree | Strongly disagree | Neither agree nor disagree | Strongly agree

Statement	Don't know	Strongly disagree	Disagree	Neither agree nor disagree	Agree	Strongly agree
I have a good understanding of 4IR technologies and their relevance for my company	0	2	11	29	54	5
My company already adopts 4IR technologies in our operations	4	2	23	30	34	7
My company plans to adopt 4IR technologies in our operations by 2025	2	2	13	29	43	13
The cost of 4IR technologies is a significant barrier to adoption for our company	5	7	18	25	43	2

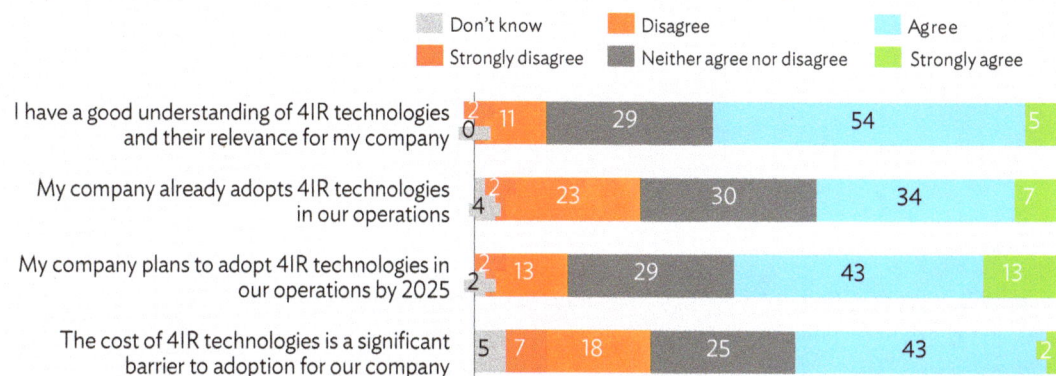

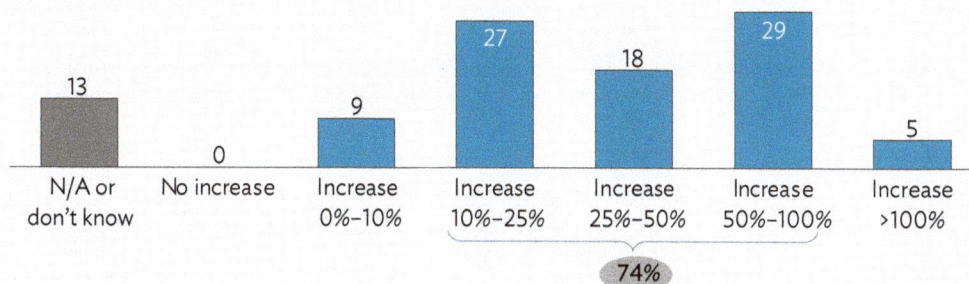

4IR = Industry 4.0 or Fourth Industrial Revolution, F&B = food and beverage.

Note: Employer survey in 2019 on impact of 4IR technology on the F&B industry in Indonesia, n=56.

Source: Asian Development Bank and AlphaBeta.

Figure 3: Expected Productivity Improvements to Indonesia's Food and Beverage Industry Due to 4IR Technology in 5 Years

F&B: Productivity

Over 70% of employers in the F&B industry expect a productivity increase of between 10%–100% from 4IR technologies over the next 5 years

Respondents (%)

Category	Value
N/A or don't know	13
No increase	0
Increase 0%–10%	9
Increase 10%–25%	27
Increase 25%–50%	18
Increase 50%–100%	29
Increase >100%	5

(Increase 10%–25% through Increase 50%–100%: 74%)

4IR = Industry 4.0 or Fourth Industrial Revolution, F&B = food and beverage.

Note: Employer survey on impact of 4IR technology on the F&B industry in Indonesia, n=56.

Source: Asian Development Bank and AlphaBeta.

(ii)   **Productivity effect**. Sometimes called a scale effect, this refers to when automation improves productivity and lowers production costs. Under normal conditions, this lowers the price of goods and services, which raises demand for them. To the extent that increased demand requires hiring more workers, it could offset the displacement effect from automation.[14]

Contrary to some perceptions that 4IR will lead to mass unemployment, the research provides an overall optimistic assessment. Net employment from 4IR may actually rise in the F&B manufacturing industry as displacement effects from 4IR are offset by employment linked to productivity gains, i.e., the income effect (Figure 4).

Figure 4: Impact of 4IR on Number of Jobs in Indonesia's Food and Beverage Industry, 2018–2013

F&B: Jobs

The overall impact of 4IR on jobs is likely to be limited as negative displacement effects are potentially offset by positive income effects

Displacement and income effects of 4IR on jobs, 2018-2030 (%)

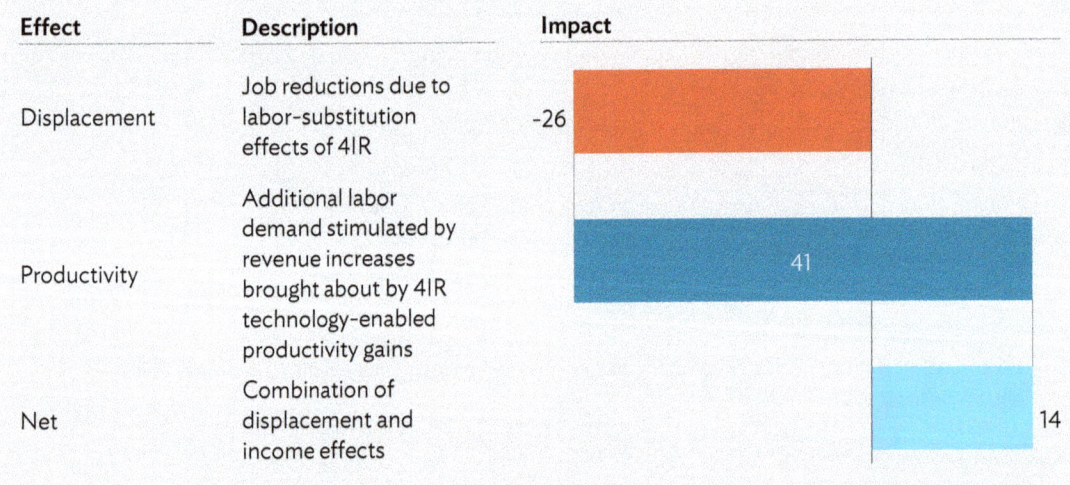

Effect	Description	Impact
Displacement	Job reductions due to labor-substitution effects of 4IR	-26
Productivity	Additional labor demand stimulated by revenue increases brought about by 4IR technology-enabled productivity gains	41
Net	Combination of displacement and income effects	14

4IR = Industry 4.0 or Fourth Industrial Revolution, F&B = food and beverage, BPS = Badan Pusat Statistik (Statistics Indonesia), GDP = gross domestic product, ILO = International Labour Organization, IMF = International Monetary Fund, IFLS = Indonesian Family Life Survey.

Note: Change in jobs based on accelerated adoption scenario of Industry 4.0 technologies.

Sources: Industry employment – BPS and ILO; GDP/Output – BPS and IMF Article IV; RAND IFLS survey data; Employer survey on impact of 4IR on the F&B industry in Indonesia, n=45+; Job portal data: jobs in the F&B industry scraped from the job portal Karir over the period from July to August 2019.

---

[14]   Automation can also spawn new labor-intensive tasks and jobs, raising demand for labor. New job categories could emerge as 4IR technologies are introduced into production, for example, or when a more sophisticated industrial robot is introduced on a factory floor and needs programming. This is referred to in the literature as the "reinstatement effect." This effect was not estimated in this analysis due to a lack of robust data to size this. Further details on the reinstatement effect can be found in ADB. 2018. *Asian Development Outlook 2018 - How Technology Affects Jobs*. https://www.adb.org/publications/asian-development-outlook-2018-how-technology-affects-jobs.

However, even though the overall impact on employment appears to be positive, this does not mean that 4IR could not lead to large groups of workers losing their jobs. There are four critical challenges to realizing the theoretical positive income effect:

(i)   There is no guarantee the 26% of workers displaced will seamlessly move into the 41% percent of jobs created. The transition may not occur if workers cannot be reskilled accordingly.

(ii)   Furthermore, the new jobs may not materialize if there is a lack of suitable skills in the local workforce to support them. In short, Indonesia's approach to skill development will be critical in realizing a positive labor market outcome related to 4IR in this industry.

(iii)   There could be potential time lags to the implementation of 4IR, job displacement, and the manifestation of productivity benefits. Hence, the productivity gains generating additional income that make new employment possible may take several years to materialize, reducing the positive impact by 2030.

(iv)   Some of the productivity benefits may be absorbed by companies as higher profits if industries are not competitive or distributed to remaining workers in higher wages if supply of labor is inelastic, meaning rather than additional employment, productivity benefits could generate higher returns for existing actors in the market.

This impact is likely to differ by occupation. For example, according to employers surveyed, manual and administrative jobs are likely to see the largest decreases due to employment as a result of 4IR technology adoption, with technical jobs seeing the largest increases (Figure 5).

Figure 5: Employers' Expected Impact of 4IR on Number of Jobs by Occupation in Indonesia's Food and Beverage Industry, 2019–2025

F&B: Jobs

With the exception of technical occupations, employers expect an overall decrease in jobs across the industry in particular for manual occupations.

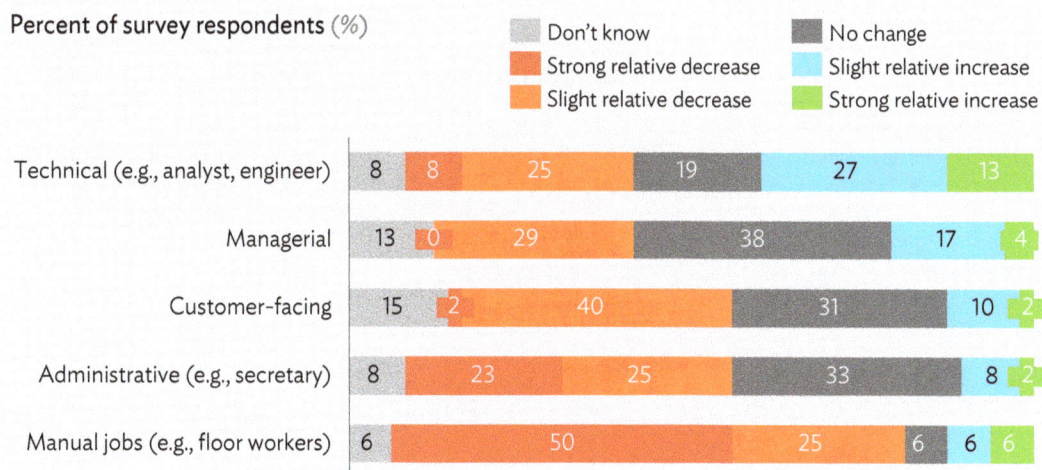

Percent of survey respondents (%)

Legend:
- Don't know
- No change
- Strong relative decrease
- Slight relative increase
- Slight relative decrease
- Strong relative increase

Occupation	Don't know	Strong relative decrease	Slight relative decrease	No change	Slight relative increase	Strong relative increase
Technical (e.g., analyst, engineer)	8	8	25	19	27	13
Managerial	13	0	29	38	17	4
Customer-facing	15	2	40	31	10	2
Administrative (e.g., secretary)	8	23	25	33	8	2
Manual jobs (e.g., floor workers)	6	50	25	6	6	6

4IR = Industry 4.0 or Fourth Industrial Revolution, F&B = food and beverage.

Source: Based on a survey and structured interviews conducted with employers in the F&B industry, n=48.

Box 1: Estimating Employment Changes

This report employs an experimental approach to understanding the impact of Industry 4.0 or the Fourth Industrial Revolution (4IR) on employment. The core data sources used in this approach are the RAND Indonesian Family Life Survey (IFLS),[a] National Labor Force Survey (LFS) Statistics publicly reported by Badan Pusat Statistik (Statistics Indonesia), online job portal data[b] and surveys of employers in the prioritized industries in Indonesia. The approach seeks to first understand how 4IR could impact the industry's growth trajectory and then how employment will change based on task shifts within occupations.

The growth trajectory of the industry is computed by looking at historic industry growth as a business-as-usual scenario and then modeling the impact of 4IR as a productivity shock that generates additional productivity growth. The assumption used for the estimates presented here is that adoption rates of 4IR technology, i.e., the number of firms in the industry that adopt a relevant mix of 4IR technologies,[c] increases to 50% until 2025 and from 2025 onward, 4IR technology adoption grows to 100% by 2030. This approach is not meant to forecast the actual, or even a necessarily realistic, level of 4IR technology adoption by 2030. Rather, it should be considered a thought experiment to understand the largest possible impact 4IR can have on employment and skills gaps. Productivity shocks and adoption levels were obtained from the employer survey and cross-referenced with the broader literature, where available.

Estimating the changes in employment across different occupations relies on a detailed analysis of task profiles (Box 2). The analysis identifies the changes in the time spent on particular tasks between today and a future in which 4IR has been adopted. Combining this with the breakdown of employment by occupation for the industry as well as the productivity growth estimates above, the result shows how different occupations may become more frequent in the industry. This part of the analysis mostly uses data from the IFLS and Indonesia's LFS.

[a] RAND. 2018. *Indonesian Family Life Survey (IFLS)*. https://www.rand.org/well-being/social-and-behavioral-policy/data/FLS/IFLS.html.
[b] The study analyzed over 180 job profiles across the food and beverage and automotive manufacturing industries, from the job portal Karir for the type and level of skills required for the job. This data was used to (i) give an accurate picture of skill demand today, and (ii) predict the trends in skill requirement changes as compared to historic data.
[c] The measure does not specify the exact mix of technologies as this can differ significantly by business. The common factor is that the firm adopts at least some technologies considered 4IR. In the consumer survey, employers were presented with a number of examples of technologies relevant to the industry. For the food and beverage manufacturing industry technologies such as Internet of Things (IoT) technologies for efficient factory production (integrating all machines and devices) and food safety (food tracking), and robotics for automation of food production were listed as examples. Respondents also highlighted additional 4IR technologies such as artificial intelligence, digital integrated human resource management, digital process monitoring and controls, digital marketing tools, e-commerce, and machine system technology. For the automotive manufacturing industry technologies such as machine inspection automation technology (machine vision), collaborative robots, cognitive computing in IoT-connected cars, and artificial intelligence for autonomous vehicles were listed as examples. Respondents also highlighted additional 4IR technologies such as 5G, augmented reality, big data, digital marketing, IoT, learning management systems, renewable energy, robotics, and virtual reality.

Source: Asian Development Bank and AlphaBeta.

Manual jobs are expected to steeply decline by 2025 as reported by 75% of employers surveyed. With potential automation and digital services, administrative and customer-facing workers will also see significant displacement. This can have consequences for gender equity. For example, in addition to the displacement of manual jobs, the F&B processing industries are likely to see significant displacement among customer-facing (approximately 29,000 workers) and administrative workers (approximately 11,000 workers). These jobs are also the occupations with the highest female–to–male ratio in the industry, approximately 37%.

To understand what drives these results, it is important to first understand that technology does not automate jobs, but rather individual or combinations of tasks. A loss of employment only occurs if automation impacts such a high share of activities associated with a job that a worker is no longer essential.

Job Task Implications

The research examines five types of tasks linked to jobs in the F&B manufacturing industry and how they could be impacted by 4IR:

(i) **Routine physical.** These tasks involve repetitive and predictable physical work. For example, a factory worker assembling parts on a manufacturing line.

(ii) **Routine interpersonal.** These tasks involve predictable interactions with other people. For example, a call center worker reading a sales script.

(iii) **Nonroutine physical.** These tasks involve physical work that is not repetitive or predictable. For example, a mechanic diagnosing and repairing problems with a car engine.

(iv) **Nonroutine interpersonal.** These tasks involve complex or creative interactions with other people. For example, supervising others or making speeches or presentations.

(v) **Analytical.** These are tasks that vary significantly and there is a strong thinking and analytical component. They predominantly involve computers or other technological equipment.

The research indicates an increase in the time spent on nonroutine interpersonal tasks as well as analytical tasks. In fact, by 2030, workers in the industry could spend an additional 13.5% of their work week on such tasks and 13.5% less time on routine physical and interpersonal tasks (Figure 6). The largest increase in time spent can be observed for nonroutine interpersonal tasks. This is likely driven by technology being able to automate routine tasks, but this will be harder for interpersonal tasks. This could also be manual workers shifting to handling customer queries, for example.

Skills Implications

The shifts in tasks influenced by 4IR will potentially have significant implications for the aggregate skills required in the industry. The study analysis considers 10 categories of skills:[15]

(i) **Critical thinking and active learning.** Skills that allow using logic and reasoning to identify the strengths and weaknesses of alternative solutions, conclusions, or approaches to problems, as well as understanding the implications of new information for both current and future problem solving and decision-making.

---

[15] The 10 skill categories and their definitions were chosen to align with the six skill groups provided by O*NET, which is one of the key databases for examining skill changes in the workforce. Some adjustments were made to the O*NET classifications to better align with the analysis. These included disaggregating O*NET's Basic Skill group into critical thinking and active learning, written and verbal communication, and numeracy; and basic digital and advanced digital/ICT skills being broken out of O*NET's broader Technical Skill group due to their particular relevance for 4IR.

Figure 6: Shifts in Time of Workers For Different Types of Tasks in Indonesia's Food and Beverage Industry, 2018–2030

F&B: Tasks

Industry 4.0 is likely to shift time spent on routine tasks to analytical and nonroutine tasks

Average share of weekly working hours spent on this task (%)

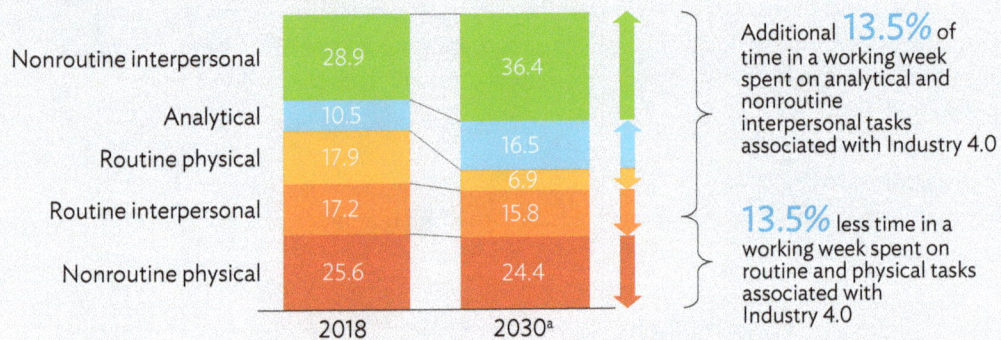

Task	2018	2030ᵃ
Nonroutine interpersonal	28.9	36.4
Analytical	10.5	16.5
Routine physical	17.9	6.9
Routine interpersonal	17.2	15.8
Nonroutine physical	25.6	24.4

Additional **13.5%** of time in a working week spent on analytical and nonroutine interpersonal tasks associated with Industry 4.0

13.5% less time in a working week spent on routine and physical tasks associated with Industry 4.0

F&B = food and beverage, BPS = Badan Pusat Statistik (Statistics Indonesia), GDP = gross domestic product, IFLS = Indonesian Family Life Survey, ILO = International Labour Organization, IMF = International Monetary Fund, LFS = Labor Force Survey.

Note: Figures include rounding adjustments.

ᵃ Based on a "high adoption" scenario of Industry 4.0.

Sources: Industry employment – BPS, LFS 2017 and ILO; GDP/Output – BPS and IMF Article IV; RAND IFLS survey data; Employer survey on impact of Industry 4.0 on the F&B industry in Indonesia, n=46+; Job portal data: jobs in the F&B industry scraped from the job portal Karir over the period from July to August 2019.

(ii)   **Written and verbal communication.** Ability to read, write, speak, and actively listen.

(iii)   **Numeracy.** Ability to use mathematics and scientific rules and methods to solve problems.

(iv)   **Complex problem solving.** Skills that help identify complex problems and review related information to develop and evaluate options and implement solutions.

(v)   **Management.** Skills that help allocate financial, material, personnel, and time resources efficiently.

(vi)   **Social.** Skills that help to work with people to achieve goals such as coordination, instructing, negotiation, persuasion, service orientation, and social perceptiveness and empathy.

(vii)   **Evaluation, judgment, and decision-making.** Skills used to understand, monitor, conduct, and improve analysis and sociotechnical systems.

(viii)   **Technical.** Skills used to design, set up, operate, maintain, and correct malfunctions involving application of machines or technological systems.

(ix)   **Computer literacy.** Skills that allow workers to effectively use computers and digital applications in their jobs, such as using email, word processing, searching the internet, data entry, and others (i.e., computer literacy skills).

(x)   **Digital/information and communication technology.** Skills to work in inherently digital occupations and perform complex tasks in a digital environment, as well as maintaining digital infrastructure such as advanced spreadsheet functions, financial software, graphic design, statistical analysis, software programming, and managing computer networks.

Box 2: Estimating Task Shifts

To analyze shifts in occupations, the study uses what the literature refers to as a task-based approach. It starts by identifying the employment breakdown of the industry according to occupations using labor force survey data. This provides an overview of the occupations in an industry and the relative employment by occupation for 43 occupations, aggregated into 5 major groups: managerial, technical (e.g., analyst, engineer), administrative (e.g., secretary), customer-facing, and manual (e.g., floor workers).

For each of the occupations in the industry, a task profile was developed. A task profile gives a detailed description of how many hours on average a week the average worker in an occupation in this industry spends executing specific tasks. Based on the literature, the five different task groups listed above were identified.[a] To create individual task profiles for each of the occupations in the relevant industries, data collected by the RAND Indonesian Family Life Survey was used. Questions from the survey were used to allocate time spent on task groups. First, the amount of time spent on routine versus nonroutine tasks was determined, then each time allocation was further split between physical, interpersonal, and analytical tasks. The result is a profile of the relative time, in terms of hours spent, of each the five task groups for each occupation in the industry.

To understand how these task profiles shift with Industry 4.0 or the Fourth Industrial Revolution (4IR) technology adoption, estimates from the employer survey were used. Employers were asked to provide estimates of the change in aggregate time spent by task in their firm (i.e., change in the total time all workers in the firm spend on the set task collectively) due to 4IR technology adoption over the next 5 years. The fundamental assumption is that the adoption of 4IR technologies changes the task profile of an occupation through automation of certain tasks and time shifted to others. This results in new task profiles by occupation for 2030 where 100% of firms have adopted 4IR.

[a] Prospera and AlphaBeta Advisors. 2019. *Capturing Indonesia's Automation Potential*. https://www.alphabeta.com/wp-content/uploads/2019/08/capturing-indonesias-automation-potential.pdf.

Source: Asian Development Bank and AlphaBeta.

Based on the skills categories above, unique current and future (i.e., post-4IR technology adoption) skill profiles for occupations in the industry were computed based on data from the World Bank STEP survey, job portal data, as well as inputs from the employer survey. These profiles were then compared to understand the skills gap created by 4IR technology adoption.

The study reveals significant changes in the skill requirements in the F&B manufacturing industry:

(i)   **Change in skills demand.** This study reviewed both employer survey data and job portal data to understand changes in the importance of skills linked to 4IR. Interestingly, while employers perceived critical thinking and active learning, complex problem solving, and technical and information and communication technology (ICT)[16] skills to be the fastest increasing skill categories, the job portal data had greater variability, and actually showed declining importance of technical and ICT skills (Figure 7).

---

[16]   Note: This represents the aggregation of the technical, computer literacy, and digital/ICT skill categories due to consistency with the available portal information.

Box 3: Estimating Skills Changes

This study used data from the World Bank Systematic Tracking of Exchanges in Procurement (STEP) survey. Indonesia is not covered by this. While skill survey data for Indonesia is available from the Organisation for Economic Co-operation and Development Survey of Adult Skills as part of the Programme for the International Assessment of Adult Competencies (PIAAC), the questionnaire is not a direct match to the STEP survey. Furthermore, out of the four focus countries, the PIAAC only covers Indonesia. To keep the skill data comparable across the focus countries, skill profiles in Indonesia's priority industries, the food and beverage manufacturing and automotive manufacturing industries, were proxied with data from the World Bank STEP survey for Viet Nam, using food and beverage processing industry; and the Philippines, using general manufacturing industry as references.

To compute current skill profiles for each occupation in the industry, data from the STEP questionnaire's Module 6: Work Skills was used. Questions from this section were used to assess the importance of each skill category. A value from a scale of 0–3 (0 for skill is not used to 3, highly advanced skills are required) was assigned to skills based on survey responses to relevant questions. The score measures both the importance and the competency level of the skill for each skill category.

Future skill profiles leveraged two sources of data: (i) data on skill and education requirements from job profiles for occupations, obtained from Indonesia's online job portals; and (ii) information about changes in skill requirements from the employer survey.

The collected job postings were analyzed in detail and assigned an importance or skill competency score (from 0 to 3) for each of the 10 skill categories. They were also categorized according to the five job groups: managerial, administrative, technical, customer-facing, and manual.

In parallel, as a second estimate, survey data of employers were leveraged to understand which skill categories would gain importance due to adoption of Industry 4.0 technologies at an industry level. Based on the responses, percentage changes in the level of importance scores were calculated for the five identified job groups. Applying these to the current skill profiles based on STEP resulted in a second set of estimates for future skills profiles.

The future skills profiles used to estimate the skills gap were then computed as an average of the two estimates and the skill gap by occupation was identified by simply examining the differences in importance scores between current and future skill profiles.

Source: World Bank. 2019. *The STEP Skills Measurement Program.* https://microdata.worldbank.org/index.php/catalog/step.

(ii) **Overall skill importance.** Evaluation, judgment, and decision-making; and critical thinking skills are likely to see their relative importance increase by 2030, replacing management skills as the most important skills in the industry (Figure 8). One reason could be that 4IR technologies will mean that less management is needed, or more detailed data, business intelligence, and artificial intelligence (AI) assistance will allow for easier management of people and resources, especially from remote locations.

(iii) **Changes in level of skills.** Overall, the industry will require significant upskilling as the demand for more intermediate and advanced skills is likely to increase (Figure 9). Interestingly, relatively few workers will require advanced level of skills; rather, most will require transitioning from a basic skill level to an intermediate skill level.

Figure 7: Potential Impact of 4IR on Shifts in Importance of Different Skills in Indonesia's Food and Beverage Industry

F&B: Skills

Evidence from job portal data does not support all employer sentiment about changes to skill importance due to 4IR adoption

Implied average change in skill importance, 2018-2025 (%)   ▢ Increase ▮ Decrease

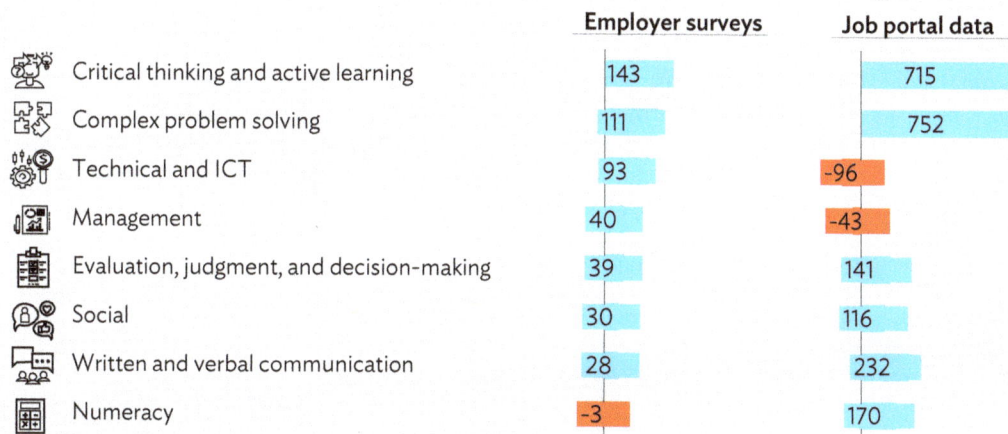

	Employer surveys	Job portal data
Critical thinking and active learning	143	715
Complex problem solving	111	752
Technical and ICT	93	-96
Management	40	-43
Evaluation, judgment, and decision-making	39	141
Social	30	116
Written and verbal communication	28	232
Numeracy	-3	170

4IR = Industry 4.0 or Fourth Industrial Revolution, F&B = food and beverage, ICT = information and communication technology, BPS = Badan Pusat Statistik (Statistics Indonesia), GDP = gross domestic product, IFLS = Indonesian Family Life Survey, ILO = International Labour Organization, IMF = International Monetary Fund, LFS = Labor Force Survey.

Sources: Industry employment – BPS, LFS 2017 and ILO; GDP/Output – BPS and IMF Article IV; RAND IFLS survey data; Employer survey on impact of 4IR on the F&B industry in Indonesia, n=46+; Job portal data: jobs in the F&B industry scraped from the job portal Karir over the period from July to August 2019.

Skills Supply Trends

Figure 10 shows the breakdown of the additional demand for training that will be required by workers in the F&B manufacturing industry under 4IR technology adoption. This reflects the volume of training required to bring the F&B workforce in Indonesia from the skills required today in 2018, to the level of skills required by 2030, driven only by 4IR technology adoption. Overall, there needs to be 51.2 million additional person training (footnote 4) by 2030. The majority of the training requirements will likely come from on-the-job training, with the rest split between short professional training and longer formal training. This also highlights the need for the formal technical and vocational education and training (TVET) industry to shift its focus from long-term training and education, to also be actively involved in shorter professional and even on-the-job training. However, the mix of training is important. Employer survey data also point to a need for boosting formal education and training to prepare graduates better for the workplace. Box 5 shows how these values were computed.

In the F&B manufacturing industry, the amount of training for workers who remain in employment (i.e., are unlikely to be displaced), but require upskilling far outweighs the number of displaced workers or even new workers entering the industry due to the net employment effect. For these workers, on-job-training might be the most suitable training type.

Box 4: Comparison of Insights in the Food and Beverage Processing Industry versus Past Research

The positive nature of the net impact on employment in the industry is in line with previous research that estimates a net positive impact by 2028. The results for the food and beverage manufacturing industry indicate larger employment gains than for manufacturing in Association of Southeast Asian Nations as a whole.

The results on tasks shifts are also in line with analysis of historical developments in tasks in the Indonesian economy, which was conducted by previous research. In particular, that analytical tasks are the fastest increasing task group in share of average time spent are similar to previous findings.

By surveying Indonesian businesses in 2016, the International Labour Organization identified technical knowledge, strategic thinking, and communication as the most critical skills for enterprises. This finding is closely aligned with the findings, in particular, the insights from job portal data that see critical thinking and communication as gaining the most importance under the Fourth Industrial Revolution. Both are also estimated to be among the top three most important skills in the food and beverage manufacturing industry by 2030 under the Industry 4.0 technology adoption.

[a] Oxford Economics. 2018. *Technology and the Future of ASEAN Jobs.*
[b] Prospera and AlphaBeta Advisors. 2019. *Capturing Indonesia's Automation Potential.* https://www.alphabeta.com/wp-content/uploads/2019/08/capturing-indonesias-automation-potential.pdf.
[c] ACT/EMP and ILO. 2017. *ASEAN in Transformation: How Technology is Changing Jobs and Enterprises: Indonesia Country Brief.* https://www.ilo.org/wcmsp5/groups/public/---ed_dialogue/---act_emp/documents/publication/wcms_579671.pdf.

Source: Asian Development Bank and AlphaBeta.

Figure 8: Impact of 4IR on Different Skills in Indonesia's Food and Beverage Industry, 2018–2030

F&B: Skills

Critical thinking skills will be much more important under 4IR while management, numeracy, and social skills are likely to be relatively less so.

Importance ranking	2018	2030
1	Management	Evaluation, judgment, and decision-making
2	Evaluation, judgment, and decision-making	Critical thinking and active learning
3	Numeracy	Written and verbal communication
4	Written and verbal communication	Numeracy
5	Technical	Management
6	Social	Complex problem solving
7	Critical thinking and active learning	Technical
8	Complex problem solving	Social
9	Computer literacy	Computer literacy
10	Digital/ICT skills	Digital/ICT skills

Skills of increasing relative importance from 2018–2030 ▮ Skills with decreasing relative importance from 2018–2030

4IR = Industry 4.0 or Fourth Industrial Revolution, F&B = food and beverage, ICT = information and communication technology, BPS = Badan Pusat Statistik (Statistics Indonesia), GDP = gross domestic product, ILO = International Labour Organization, IMF = International Monetary Fund, LFS = Labor Force Survey.

Sources: Industry employment – BPS, LFS 2017 and ILO; GDP/Output – BPS and IMF Article IV; RAND IFLS survey data; Employer survey on impact of 4IR on the F&B industry in Indonesia, n=40+; Job portal data: jobs in the F&B industry scraped from the job portal Karir over the period from July to August 2019.

Figure 9: Impact of 4IR Adoption on Level of Skills Required in Indonesia's Food and Beverage Industry, 2018–2030

F&B: Skills

4IR adoption will require large increases in intermediate skills as well as basic computer and digital skills.

Skills	Absolute change in percentage of workers requiring skill at level (2018–2030)		
	Basic (%)	Intermediate (%)	Advanced (%)
Critical thinking and active learning	(3.0)	93.3	6.1
Written and verbal communication	(97.3)	92.9	4.4
Numeracy	(96.3)	96.3	0.0
Complex problem solving	2.6	93.9	0.7
Management	(93.7)	93.0	0.7
Social	(1.8)	(1.8)	3.6
Evaluation, judgment, and decision-making	(93.7)	(6.3)	100.0
Technical	(87.6)	92.9	1.1
Computer literacy	95.7	0.8	0.7
Digital/ICT skills	98.9	1.1	0.0

Legend:
- >50%
- >10%
- ≤10%; ≥−10%
- < −10%
- < −50%

( ) = negative, 4IR = Industry 4.0 or Fourth Industrial Revolution, F&B = food and beverage, ICT = information and communication technology, BPS = Badan Pusat Statistik (Statistics Indonesia), GDP = gross domestic product, IFLS = Indonesian Family Life Survey, ILO = International Labour Organization, IMF = International Monetary Fund, LFS = Labor Force Survey.

Sources: Industry employment – BPS, LFS 2017 and ILO; GDP/Output – BPS and IMF Article IV; RAND IFLS survey data; Employer survey on impact of 4IR on the F&B industry in Indonesia, n=19+; Job portal data: jobs in the F&B industry scraped from the job portal Karir over the period from July to August 2019.

To better understand Indonesia's training and education industry, two surveys were conducted. As part of the survey of employers in the F&B manufacturing industry, respondents were asked to comment on their ability to attract good candidates for jobs as well as their current engagement in training efforts. Further, a separate training institute survey was commissioned, the results of which are discussed in Chapter 2.

Survey results of employers in the F&B manufacturing industry reveal that about 29% of employers have difficulties identifying high-quality graduates (Figure 11). Of the employers, 31% also expressed concerns about the how prepared graduates were for their jobs by their previous education or training, data pointing to a lack of job-specific skills. This is echoed by insights from industry sources, shared during country consultations, who highlighted significant challenges in finding suitably qualified graduates.

Figure 10: Additional Training Required to Meet Skills Demand from Industry 4.0 Adoption in Indonesia's Food and Beverage Industry, by Training Channel, 2030

F&B: Training

Fifty percent of the additional demand for training driven by Industry 4.0 adoption will likely need to be met by on-the-job training.

Millions of person trainings required by channel[a]

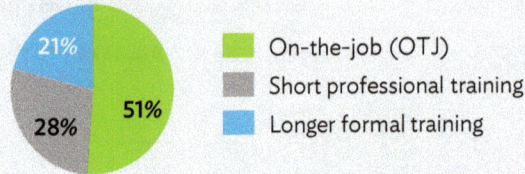

- 51% On-the-job (OTJ)
- 28% Short professional training
- 21% Longer formal training

BPS = Badan Pusat Statistik (Statistics Indonesia), GDP = gross domestic product, IFLS = Indonesian Family Life Survey, ILO = International Labour Organization, IMF = International Monetary Fund, LFS = Labor Force Survey.

Notes:

1. Figures include rounding adjustments.
2. One-person training refers to training one worker in one skill from the level required by his or her occupation's skill profile in 2018 to the relevant level given by the skills profile in 2030.

[a]   On-the-job training refers to training conducted during day to day such as senior staff instructing junior staff or running internal seminars; Short professional training refers to short (between 1 day to 6 months) courses conducted by professional internal or external instructors (e.g., weekend seminars, boot-camps); Longer formal trainings refer to trainings longer than 6 months for which workers would likely have to take leave from their jobs, these include returning into formal education such as obtaining a degree.

Sources: Industry employment – BPS, LFS 2017 and ILO; GDP/Output – BPS and IMF Article IV; RAND IFLS survey data; Employer survey on impact of 4IR on the F&B industry in Indonesia, n=40+; Job portal data: jobs in the F&B industry scraped from the job portal Karir.

Figure 11: Employer Sentiment in Indonesia's Food and Beverage Industry Toward Graduates Hired in the Past 24 Months

F&B: Supply

Almost a third of employers in the F&B industry feel identifying high quality graduates is not easy and graduates are inadequately prepared.

Respondents, (%)

Legend: Don't know | Disagree | Agree | Strongly disagree | Neither agree nor disagree | Strongly agree

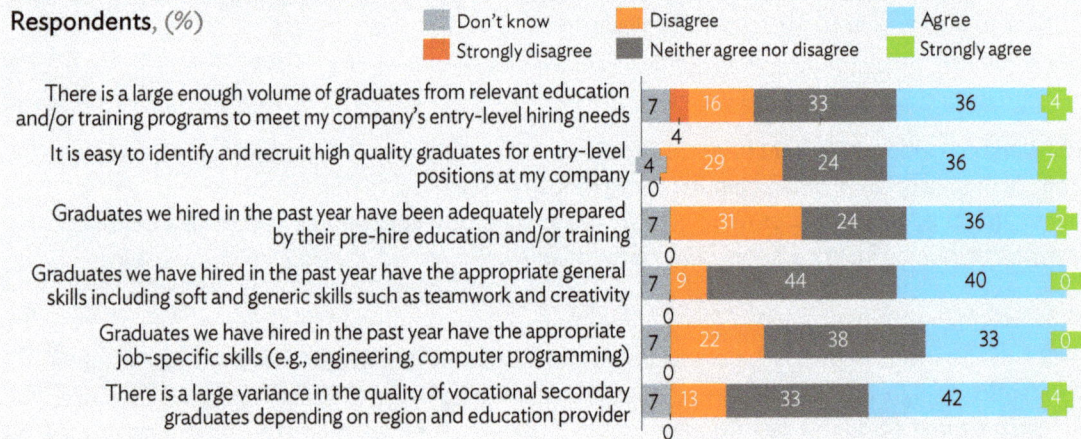

Statement	Strongly disagree	Disagree	Neither agree nor disagree	Agree	Strongly agree	Don't know
There is a large enough volume of graduates from relevant education and/or training programs to meet my company's entry-level hiring needs	7	16	33	36	4	4
It is easy to identify and recruit high quality graduates for entry-level positions at my company	4	29	24	36	7	0
Graduates we hired in the past year have been adequately prepared by their pre-hire education and/or training	7	31	24	36	2	0
Graduates we have hired in the past year have the appropriate general skills including soft and generic skills such as teamwork and creativity	7	9	44	40	0	0
Graduates we have hired in the past year have the appropriate job-specific skills (e.g., engineering, computer programming)	7	22	38	33	0	0
There is a large variance in the quality of vocational secondary graduates depending on region and education provider	7	13	33	42	4	0

F&B = food and beverage.

Source: Employer survey on impact of the Fourth Industrial Revolution on the F&B industry in Indonesia, n=45.

Box 5: Estimating Training Requirements

Skill supply, or in other words, training requirement, can be quantified in person training. One-person training refers to training one worker in one skill from the skill level specified by the person's occupation skill profile in the industry, in 2018, to the required level under Fourth Industrial Revolution (4IR) technology adoption. Hence, the training required to shift a worker from the worker's current skill profile, to the future skill profile would require one-person training per skill that needs improvement between 2018 and 2030.

To understand the type of training needed, in particular, the length of training, two factors need to be considered: (i) understanding the level of skill improvement needed, and (ii) understanding the access to different training channels by different workers.

Individuals' training needs are going to differ if they require an improvement of skills from basic to intermediate levels, intermediate to advanced levels, or even basic to advanced levels. For example, a worker who only requires basic technical skills today, but requires advanced technical skills in 2030 under 4IR technology adoption will likely require more training than another worker who only has to improve skills from intermediate to advanced. Same goes for workers who do not need a particular skill today, but will require it in 2030, whether basic, intermediate, or advanced.

Apart from the length of training required to obtain a certain level of skills, the access to different channels of training may not be the same for all workers in the industry. For example, workers displaced from their jobs may not be able to receive on-the-job training, but require formal training prior to being able to find new employment. Similarly, for future generations of workers (i.e., students currently in formal education or training) it may make more sense to embed skill training in their formal curriculum, rather than waiting to train them on-the-job. Three categories of workers impacted by Industry 4.0 or the 4IR were identified based on the skill demand analysis:

- **Workers in need of reskilling.** These workers will likely lose their current jobs due to automation, meaning they need to receive training that makes them employable in new jobs created.
- **Workers in need of upskilling.** These workers will likely remain in their occupations, but the adoption of 4IR technologies means they will have to acquire new skills as well as advance existing skills to upgrade to their occupation's future skill profile.
- **Future workers.** These will be additional workers required to fill the jobs generated from growing demand. Hence, they are workers that did not previously work in the industry, but could either join as new graduates or professional hires from other industries.

The distinction of the type of worker is important as different workers have access to different types of training. For example, while future workers are likely to receive some of their skill training in the formal education industry, returning to formal education is an unlikely option for workers in need of upskilling, who will continue to be employed during their training.

Source: Asian Development Bank and AlphaBeta.

Automotive Manufacturing Industry

The findings for the automotive manufacturing industry are broadly consistent with those of the F&B manufacturing industry. Similar to the F&B manufacturing industry, the overall impact on employment is estimated to be net positive driven by strong productivity gains associated with 4IR. The automation impact is likely to be felt mainly for manual jobs.

Interestingly, the automotive manufacturing industry is expected to see a reduction in all physical tasks (routine and nonroutine), with a significant increase in analytical tasks. In contrast, the F&B manufacturing industry showed a slight increase in nonroutine physical tasks. This is consistent with the high penetration of robotics on automotive assembly lines. In terms of skills, as in the F&B manufacturing industry, judgment and decision-making, and critical thinking and active learning skills will become more important by 2030. Overall, there needs to be 1 million additional person training (footnote 4) by 2030, the majority of which could be by on-the-job training.

Relevance of Industry 4.0

The automotive manufacturing industry was at the forefront of the second Industrial Revolution, when Henry Ford introduced the assembly line concept in 1913. 4IR promises similar transformative benefits for the automotive manufacturing industry, and this industry has been one of the strongest adopters of 4IR technologies to date. There are several macroeconomic drivers supporting this shift to 4IR in the automotive manufacturing industry. These include:

(i) **A need for more flexible supply options.** As demand shifts to emerging markets, many emerging nations are not large enough for multiple original equipment manufacturers to reach sustainable scales in production. New technologies can enable plants with innovative, stripped-down designs that dramatically lower construction costs, which are traditionally a large share of car production costs.

(ii) **Global supply chains.** Automotive manufacturers have locations all over the world and 4IR technologies can enable seamless connectivity between these locations to enable operations to shift in response to production or demand fluctuations.

(iii) **Changing consumer trends.** Consumers are increasingly demanding more customization of vehicles. 4IR technologies can enable auto manufacturers to customize individual vehicles and shorten delivery times.

(iv) **Shifting regulatory trends**. Both suppliers and original equipment manufacturers in the automotive manufacturing industry are subject to increasingly stringent fuel regulations, which requires quickly adapting to manufacturing specifications (e.g., light weighting of vehicles), and 4IR technologies can support this agility in production systems.

(v) **Greater focus on reliability of production systems.** As facilities increasingly move toward 24-hour production, equipment reliability becomes even more critical. 4IR-enabled plants have robust monitoring systems to identify potential maintenance issues before they cause downtime.

(vi) **Talent shortages.** Challenges in recruitment of talent, particularly related to technicians, skilled trades workers, and engineers, combined with cost pressures, are driving shifts toward automation.

There are various 4IR technologies of relevance for the automotive manufacturing industry, ranging from digital technologies supporting autonomous vehicles through to technologies transforming the production system. The Boston Consulting Group estimated that 4IR technologies could create productivity gains equivalent to 6% to 9% of manufacturing costs in the automotive manufacturing sector.[17]

Some key technologies include:

(i)   **Internet of Things.** IoT refers to networks of sensors and actuators embedded in machines and other physical objects that connect with one another and the internet. It has a wide range of applications, including data collection, monitoring, decision-making, and process optimization (footnote 13). For example, Bosch realized a 25% increase in output for its automatic braking system and electronic stability program, simply by introducing smart, connected lines.[18]

(ii)   **Artificial intelligence and big data.** Big data refers to the ability to analyze extremely large volumes of data, extract insights, and act on them closer to real time. This has a range of benefits in the automotive manufacturing industry, including being able to use predictive analytics to fine-tune production volumes and processes, better supply chain management, and greater insights on customer segments.

(iii)   **Industry robotics.** Industrial robots have been used for a long time in the automotive manufacturing industry, but today they are becoming more autonomous and flexible. In the People's Republic of China, there are over 500 robots per 10,000 employees in the automotive manufacturing industry.[19] This is driven by a combination of factors, including advancements in robotic functions, the need for 24 x 7 production systems, and rising wages.

(iv)   **Additive manufacturing.** This describes the technologies that build 3D objects by adding layer-upon-layer of material. Additive manufacturing allows for the creation of bespoke parts with complex geometries and little wastage. Additive manufacturing is particularly valuable in the automotive manufacturing industry due to faster development cycles, part consolidation, light-weighting, and new and custom geometries.[20]

Of the businesses surveyed in the automotive manufacturing industry, 78% say they have a good understanding of of these technologies' relevance to their industry (Figure 12). Of these, 48% agree they are already adopting 4IR technologies to some degree and 12% are planning to adopt 4IR over the next 5 years. However, there are concerns about the cost of 4IR technology adoption as 46% of employers see the cost as a significant barrier.

The likely reason employers in the automotive manufacturing industry are eager to adopt 4IR is a general belief of high productivity returns. According to the survey data, over 75% of employers in Indonesia's automotive manufacturing industry believe the productivity improvements their industry can expect from 4IR over the next 5 years to be greater than 25%. Moreover, 46% of employers anticipate productivity increase of as much as 50% and above. (Figure 13). This is in line with research published by McKinsey & Company mentioned previously (footnote 6).

---

[17]   Boston Consulting Group. 2015. *Industry 4.0: The Future of Productivity and Growth in Manufacturing Industries.* https://www.bcg.com/publications/2015/engineered_products_project_business_industry_4_future_productivity_growth_manufacturing_industries.

[18]   K. Masters. 2015. The Impact of Industry 4.0 on the Automotive Manufacturing Industry. *Flexis blog.* https://blog.flexis.com/the-impact-of-industry-4-0-on-the-automotive-industry.

[19]   International Federation of Robotics (IFR). 2019. Why Robot Sales in China will Survive Slowdown in Car Production. *IFR blog.* https://ifr.org/post/Why-robot-sales-in-China-will-survive-slowdown-in-car-production.

[20]   S. Goehrke. 2018. Additive Manufacturing is Driving the Future of the Automotive Manufacturing Industry. *Forbes.* https://www.forbes.com/sites/sarahgoehrke/2018/12/05/additive-manufacturing-is-driving-the-future-of-the-automotive-industry/#2eb708e775cc.

Figure 12: Sentiment Toward Industry 4.0 in Indonesia's Automotive Industry

Automotive: 4IR readiness

Companies in the automotive industry claim to have a good understanding of 4IR but adoption is somewhat limited.

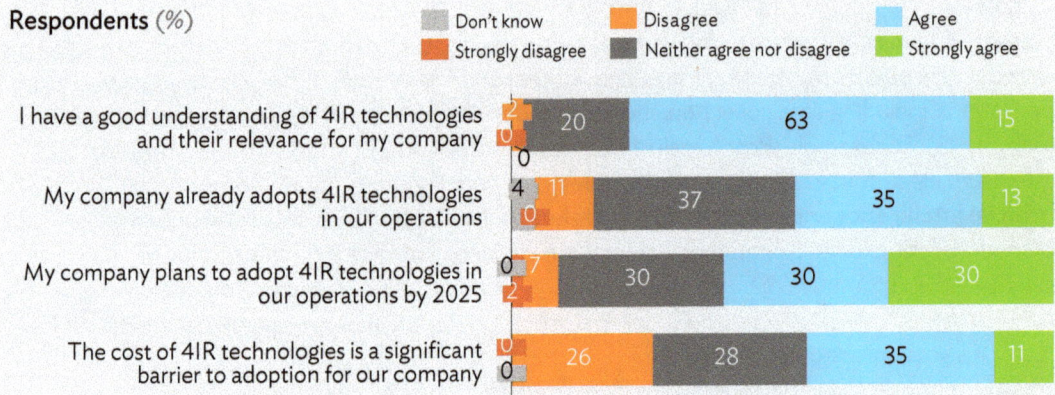

Respondents (%)

Legend: Don't know | Disagree | Agree | Strongly disagree | Neither agree nor disagree | Strongly agree

- I have a good understanding of 4IR technologies and their relevance for my company: 2, 0, 0, 20, 63, 15
- My company already adopts 4IR technologies in our operations: 4, 11, 0, 37, 35, 13
- My company plans to adopt 4IR technologies in our operations by 2025: 0, 7, 2, 30, 30, 30
- The cost of 4IR technologies is a significant barrier to adoption for our company: 0, 26, 0, 28, 35, 11

4IR = Industry 4.0 or Fourth Industrial Revolution.

Source: Employer survey on impact of 4IR on the Automotive industry in Indonesia, n=46.

Figure 13: Expected Automotive Industry Productivity Improvement in Indonesia Due to 4IR Technologies in 5 Years

Automotive: Jobs

Over 75% of employers in the automotive industry expect a productivity increase by over 25% from 4IR technologies over the next 5 years.

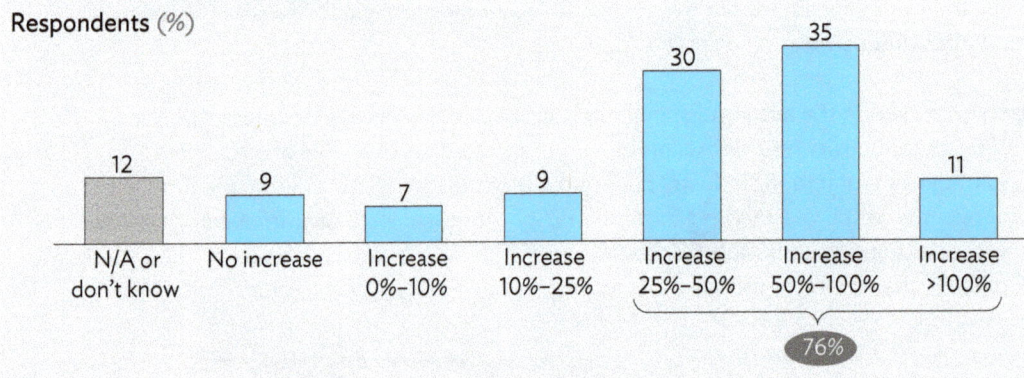

Respondents (%)

- N/A or don't know: 12
- No increase: 9
- Increase 0%–10%: 7
- Increase 10%–25%: 9
- Increase 25%–50%: 30
- Increase 50%–100%: 35
- Increase >100%: 11

76%

4IR = Industry 4.0 or Fourth Industrial Revolution, N/A = not available.

Source: Employer survey on impact of 4IR on the Automotive industry in Indonesia, n=41.

Skills Demand Analysis

Employment Implications

The findings for the automotive manufacturing industry are similar to those observed in the F&B manufacturing industry (Figure 14). Approximately 29% of jobs are likely to be displaced and 30% additional labor demand is expected to be stimulated through 4IR. The overall effect on employment is likely to be net positive with an increase of around 1% of current jobs predicted by 2030 due to 4IR.

The automotive industry will face the same challenges as the F&B manufacturing industry to realize the positive income effect from the application of 4IR. Indonesia's approach to skill development will be critical in realizing a positive labor market outcome related to 4IR. Displaced workers will be able to seamlessly move into newly created jobs only with adequate skills needed by the industry.

The displacement impact of 4IR on the automotive manufacturing industry is likely to be evenly distributed among men and women with approximately 26,000 male and 20,000 female jobs at risk.

Figure 14: Impact of 4IR on Number of Jobs in Indonesia's Automotive Industry, 2018–2030

Automotive: Jobs

The overall impact of 4IR on jobs is likely to be marginally positive as displacement is potentially offset by income effects.

Displacement and income effects of 4IR on jobs, 2018–2030 (%)

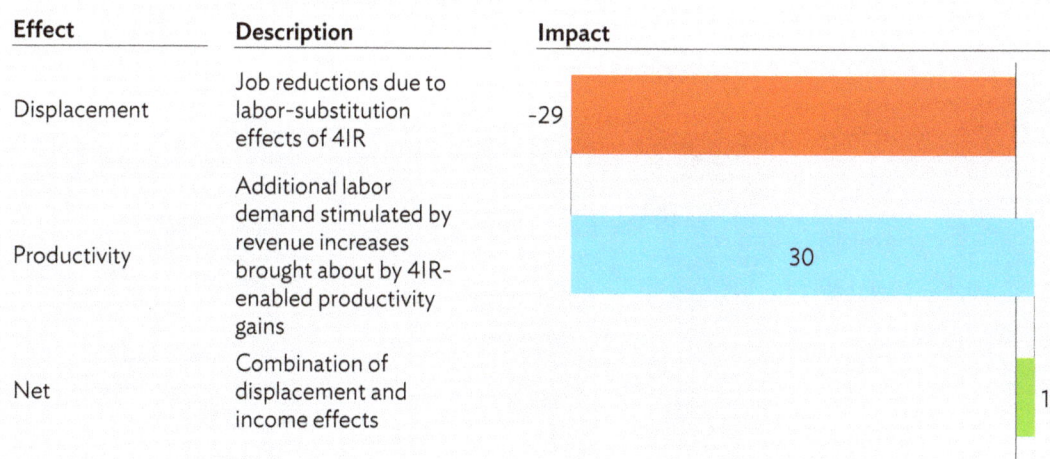

Effect	Description	Impact
Displacement	Job reductions due to labor-substitution effects of 4IR	-29
Productivity	Additional labor demand stimulated by revenue increases brought about by 4IR-enabled productivity gains	30
Net	Combination of displacement and income effects	1

4IR = Industry 4.0 or Fourth Industrial Revolution, BPS = Badan Pusat Statistik (Statistics Indonesia), GDP = gross domestic product, IFLS = Indonesian Family Life Survey, ILO = International Labour Organization, IMF = International Monetary Fund, LFS = Labor Force Survey.

Note: Change in jobs based on accelerated adoption scenario of 4IR technologies.

Sources: Industry employment – BPS, LFS 2017 and ILO; GDP/Output – BPS, McKinsey and IMF Article IV; RAND IFLS survey data; Employer survey on impact of 4IR on the Automotive industry in Indonesia, n=29; Job portal data: jobs in the Automotive industry scraped from the job portal Karir over the period from July to August 2019.

Job Task Implications

On aggregate, a larger task shift is expected for the automotive manufacturing industry as opposed to the F&B manufacturing industry (Figure 15). According to the results, workers in the industry could spend an additional 9.5% of time in a working week on analytical and interpersonal tasks associated with 4IR, and less time on physical tasks (both routine and nonroutine).

This is consistent with insights from the employer survey, with 83% of employers expecting routine physical tasks to decline in the future (Figure 16).

Skills Implications

The analysis highlights some significant changes in the industry's skill requirements:

(i)   **Change in skills demand.** According to employers, digital and ICT skills, technical and critical thinking skills will see the biggest increases in importance over the next 5 years. This is in contrast with data extracted from online job portals (Figure 17). According to online job portal data collected for this research, digital, and technical skills are likely to decline in importance,

---

Figure 15: Shifts in Time Spent by Workers on Different Types of Tasks in Indonesia's Automotive Industry, 2018–2030

Automotive: Tasks

4IR application in the automotive industry could potentially lead to a substantial reduction in the time spent on physical tasks.

Average share of weekly working hours spent on this task (%)

Task	2018	2030[a]
Nonroutine interpersonal	27.1	31.8
Analytical	9.6	14.4
Routine interpersonal	18.4	18.4
Routine physical	19.4	12.2
Nonroutine physical	25.5	23.2

Additional 9.5% of time in a working week spent on analytical and interpersonal tasks associated with Industry 4.0

9.5% less time in a working week spent on physical tasks associated with Industry 4.0

4IR = Industry 4.0 or Fourth Industrial Revolution, BPS = Badan Pusat Statistik (Statistics Indonesia), GDP = gross domestic product, IFLS = Indonesian Family Life Survey, ILO = International Labour Organization, IMF = International Monetary Fund, LFS = Labor Force Survey.

Note: Figures include rounding adjustments

a   Based on a high adoption scenario of 4IR. Emerging trends alignment.

Sources: Industry employment – BPS, LFS 2017 and ILO; GDP/Output – BPS, McKinsey and IMF Article IV; RAND IFLS survey data; Employer survey on impact of 4IR on the Automotive industry in Indonesia, n=29; Job portal data: jobs in the Automotive industry scraped from the job portal Karir over the period from July to August 2019.

Figure 16: Employers' Expected Impact of 4IR on Working Time Spent on Different Tasks in Indonesia's Automotive Industry, 2018–2030

Automotive: Tasks

The majority of employers believes that the frequency of all but analytical tasks will decrease by 4IR adoption.

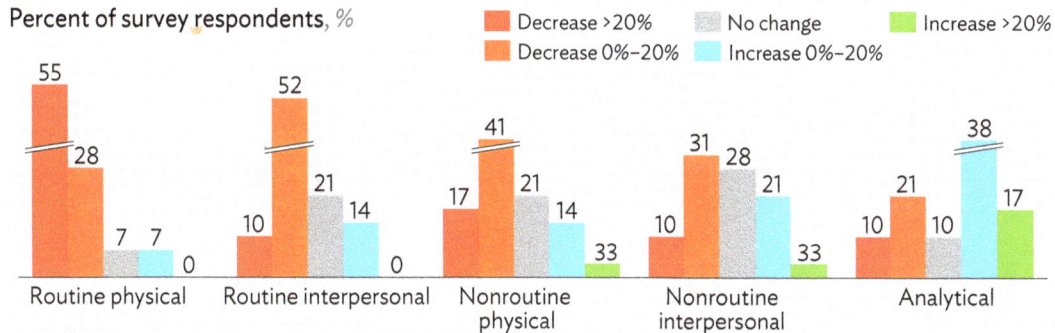

Percent of survey respondents, %

Legend:
- Decrease >20%
- Decrease 0%–20%
- No change
- Increase 0%–20%
- Increase >20%

	Routine physical	Routine interpersonal	Nonroutine physical	Nonroutine interpersonal	Analytical
Decrease >20%	55	52	17	10	10
Decrease 0%–20%	28	10	41	31	21
No change	7	21	21	28	10
Increase 0%–20%	7	14	14	21	38
Increase >20%	0	0	33	33	17

4IR = Industry 4.0 or Fourth Industrial Revolution.

Note: Answers in above chart do not sum to 100% as figure for the response "Don't know" was not included.

Source: Employer survey on impact of 4IR on the Automotive industry in Indonesia, n=29.

Figure 17: Potential Impact of 4IR on Shifts in Importance of Different Skills in Indonesia's Automotive industry

Automotive: Skills

As opposed to employers, job portal data do not indicate digital skills as becoming more important, in fact the opposite is the case.

Implied average change in skill importance, 2018–2025 (%)

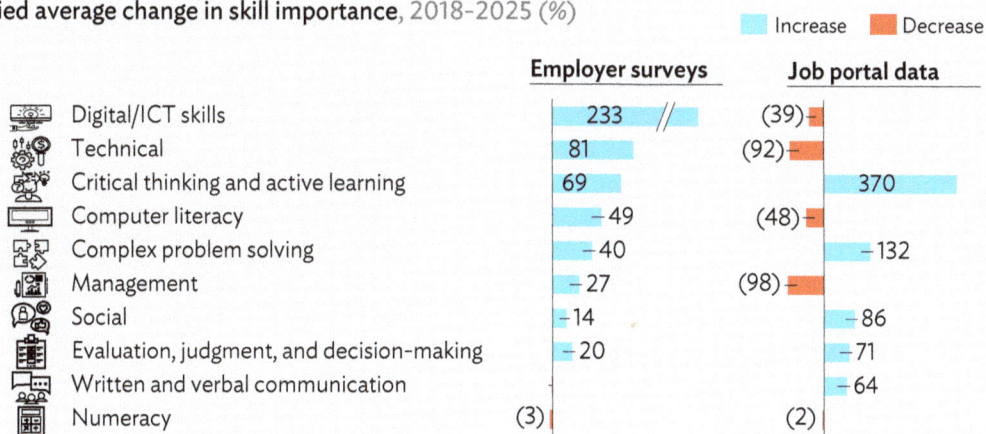

Legend: Increase / Decrease

	Employer surveys	Job portal data
Digital/ICT skills	233	(39)
Technical	81	(92)
Critical thinking and active learning	69	370
Computer literacy	49	(48)
Complex problem solving	40	132
Management	27	(98)
Social	14	86
Evaluation, judgment, and decision-making	20	71
Written and verbal communication		64
Numeracy	(3)	(2)

( ) = negative, 4IR = Industry 4.0 or Fourth Industrial Revolution, F&B = food and beverage, ICT = information and communication technology, BPS = Badan Pusat Statistik (Statistics Indonesia), GDP = gross domestic product, IFLS = Indonesian Family Life Survey, ILO = International Labour Organization, IMF = International Monetary Fund, LFS = Labor Force Survey.

Sources: Industry employment – BPS, LFS 2017 and ILO; GDP/Output – BPS, McKinsey and IMF Article IV; RAND IFLS survey data; Employer survey on impact of 4IR on the Automotive industry in Indonesia, n=29; Job portal data: jobs in the automotive industry scraped from the job portal Karir over the period from July to August 2019.

while critical thinking and complex problem solving will be the most important skills under 4IR. Different from the F&B manufacturing industry, the job portal data also predicts that numeracy is unlikely to increase in importance.

(ii)   **Overall skill importance.** Similar to the F&B manufacturing industry, judgment and decision-making, and critical thinking and active learning skills will likely be the most important skills by 2030 due to 4IR technology adoption (Figure 18). Written and verbal communication and management skills are forecast to decline in relative importance.

(iii)   **Changes in level of skills.** In contrast to the F&B manufacturing industry, the automotive manufacturing industry is less likely to experience major increases in the number of workers requiring intermediate-level skills (Figure 19). Only evaluation, judgment, and decision-making; and social skills are likely to be required at advanced levels. Furthermore, almost all workers in the automotive manufacturing industry will need to acquire basic digital skills by 2030 as a result of 4IR technology adoption, rather than just basic computer literacy, which is the case today.

Figure 18: Impact of 4IR on Importance of Different Skills in Indonesia's Automotive Industry, 2018–2030

Automotive: Skills

The list of most important skills in the automotive industry is likely to change due to 4IR technology adoption.

Skills of increasing relative importance from 2018–2030
Skills with decreasing relative importance from 2018–2030

Importance ranking	2018	2030
1	Management	Evaluation, judgment, and decision-making
2	Written and verbal communication	Social
3	Evaluation, judgment, and decision-making	Critical thinking and active learning
4	Numeracy	Written and verbal communication
5	Social	Computer literacy
6	Computer literacy	Management
7	Technical	Numeracy
8	Complex problem solving	Complex problem solving
9	Critical thinking and active learning	Technical
10	Digital/ICT skills	Digital/ICT skills

4IR = Industry 4.0 or Fourth Industrial Revolution, ICT = information and communication technology, BPS = Badan Pusat Statistik (Statistics Indonesia), GDP = gross domestic product, IFLS = Indonesian Family Life Survey, ILO = International Labour Organization, IMF = International Monetary Fund, LFS = Labor Force Survey.

Sources: Industry employment – BPS, LFS 2017 and ILO; GDP/Output – BPS, McKinsey and IMF Article IV; RAND IFLS survey data; Employer survey on impact of 4IR on the Automotive industry in Indonesia, n=29; Job portal data: jobs in the Automotive industry scraped from the job portal Karir over the period from July to August 2019.

Box 6: Comparison of Insights in the Automotive Manufacturing Industry versus Past Research

According to the International Labour Organization (ILO), about 58% of jobs in the automotive manufacturing industry are at high risk of automation, which is almost double the displacement impact estimated in this report.[a] Therefore, this report is more optimistic on the impact of Industry 4.0 or the Fourth Industrial Revolution (4IR) on the industry, in particular, if the positive income effect is considered.

However, the finding that any positive impact on employment from 4IR in the automotive manufacturing industry may be rather marginal (i.e., 1%) are similar to previous findings from the Asian Development Bank and Indonesia's National Development Planning Agency (BAPPENAS). A survey of medium and large manufacturing firms showed that for high-tech industries, which covers the manufacture of machinery, value added increased over the duration of the survey, 2000–2013, partially due to technological advances, but employment had not.[b] Similar to the findings here, productivity advances did not lead to additional hiring, however, some of the impact may have led to increasing wages.[c]

The insights on skill shifts in the automotive manufacturing industry are also largely consistent with the ILO analysis discussed in Box 1, but there are some noticeable differences. The ILO identified technical knowledge, strategic thinking, and communication as the most critical skills for enterprises. Yet, communication skills are estimated to lose importance in the automotive manufacturing industry. However, social skills, of which teamwork is a subcomponent, are increasing in importance to become the second most important skill by 2030 under 4IR technology adoption. Teamwork was identified by the ILO as the fourth most critical skill in 2016 for Indonesian enterprises.

Critical thinking and complex problem solving and systems analysis[d] were also identified as key skill needs for future investment under Work Readiness skills by the United States Agency for International Development.[e]

[a] ACT/EMP and ILO. 2017. *ASEAN in Transformation: How Technology is Changing Jobs and Enterprises: Indonesia Country Brief.* https://www.ilo.org/wcmsp5/groups/public/---ed_dialogue/---act_emp/documents/publication/wcms_579671.pdf.
[b] Asian Development Bank (ADB) and BAPPENAS. 2019. *Policies to Support the Development of Indonesia's Manufacturing Industry during 2020–2024.* https://www.adb.org/publications/policies-manufacturing-sector-indonesia-2020-2024.
[c] ADB. 2013. *Technological Change, Skill Demand, and Wage Inequality in Indonesia.* https://www.adb.org/publications/technological-change-skill-demand-and-wage-inequality-indonesia.
[d] Captured in this analysis under evaluation, judgment, and decision-making.
[e] USAID and FHI. 2015. *Workforce Connections – Analysis of Skills Demand in Indonesia.* https://www.fhi360.org/sites/default/files/media/documents/resource-skills-analysis-indonesia.pdf.

Source: Asian Development Bank and AlphaBeta.

Figure 19: Impact of 4IR on the Level of Skills Required in Indonesia's Automotive Industry, 2018–2030

Automotive: Skills

Only evaluation and social skills are likely to be required at advanced levels in the automotive industry.

Skills	Absolute change in percentage of workers requiring skill at level, 2018–2030		
	Basic (%)	Intermediate (%)	Advanced (%)
Critical thinking and active learning	(100.0)	92.0	8.0
Written and verbal communication	0.0	(3.4)	3.4
Numeracy	0.0	0.0	0.0
Complex problem solving	(13.4)	11.5	2.0
Management	0.0	(1.4)	1.4
Social	0.0	(100.0)	100.0
Evaluation, judgment, and decision-making	0.0	(100.0)	100.0
Technical	0.5	1.4	2.0
Computer literacy	(96.9)	94.9	2.0
Digital/ICT skills	93.5	3.4	0.0

Legend:
- >50%
- >10%
- ≤10%; ≥-10%
- < -10%
- < -50%

( ) = negative, 4IR = Industry 4.0 or Fourth Industrial Revolution, ICT = information and communication technology, BPS = Badan Pusat Statistik (Statistics Indonesia), GDP = gross domestic product, IFLS = Indonesian Family Life Survey, ILO = International Labour Organization, IMF = International Monetary Fund, LFS = Labor Force Survey.

Sources: Industry employment – BPS, LFS 2017 and ILO; GDP/Output – BPS, McKinsey and IMF Article IV; RAND IFLS survey data; Employer survey on impact of 4IR on the Automotive industry in Indonesia, n=29; Job portal data: jobs in the Automotive industry scraped from the job portal Karir over the period from July to August 2019.

Skills Supply Trends

Figure 20 shows the breakdown of the additional demand for training workers in the automotive manufacturing industry will require under 4IR technology adoption. This reflects the volume of training required to bring the automotive workforce in Indonesia from the skills required today in 2018, to the level of skills required by 2030, driven only by 4IR technology adoption. Overall, there needs to be 1 million additional person training (footnote 4) by 2030. Similar to the F&B manufacturing industry, the majority of the required skills development needs to come from on-the-job training.

Over 40% of surveyed employers disagreed that fresh graduates were adequately prepared for the entry-level jobs (Figure 21). In particular, employers disagreed that graduates had the right job-specific skills to adequately prepare them for the automotive manufacturing industry. Furthermore, close to 70% of employers agree or strongly agree that the quality of graduates can vary largely between regions and education providers.

Figure 20: Additional Person Training Required to Meet Skills Demand from 4IR Adoption in Indonesia's Automotive Industry, by Training Channel, 2030

Automotive: Skills

The majority of demand for training driven by 4IR adoption will likely need to be serviced by on-the-job training.

Millions of person trainings required by channel

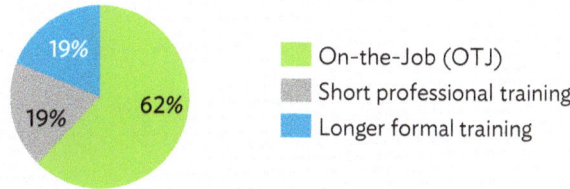

- On-the-Job (OTJ)
- Short professional training
- Longer formal training

19% / 19% / 62%

4IR = Industry 4.0 or Fourth Industrial Revolution, BPS = Badan Pusat Statistik (Statistics Indonesia), GDP = gross domestic product, IFLS = Indonesian Family Life Survey, ILO = International Labour Organization, IMF = International Monetary Fund, LFS = Labor Force Survey.

Notes:
1. Figures include rounding adjustments.
2. One-person training refers to training one worker in one skill from the level required by his or her occupation's skill profile in 2018 to the relevant level given by the skills profile in 2030.
3. On-the-job training refers to training conducted during day to day such as senior staff instructing junior staff or running internal seminars; short professional training refers to short (1 day to 6 months) courses conducted by professional internal or external instructors (e.g., weekend seminars, boot-camps); and longer formal trainings refer to trainings longer than 6 months for which workers would likely have to take leave from their jobs—these include returning into formal education such as obtaining a degree.

LFS Sources: Industry employment – BPS, Labor Force Survey 2017 and ILO; GDP/Output – BPS, McKinsey and IMF Article IV; RAND IFLS survey data; Employer survey on impact of 4IR on the Automotive industry in Indonesia, n=29; Job portal data: jobs in the Automotive industry scraped from the job portal Karir over the period from July to August 2019.

Figure 21: Indonesia Employer Sentiment Toward Graduates Hired in the Past 2 Years

Automotive: Supply

Over 40 of employers feel that hires are not prepared for entry positions, likely due to a lack of job-specific skills, and quality varies widely.

Respondents (%)

- Don't know
- Strongly disagree
- Disagree
- Neither agree nor disagree
- Agree
- Strongly agree

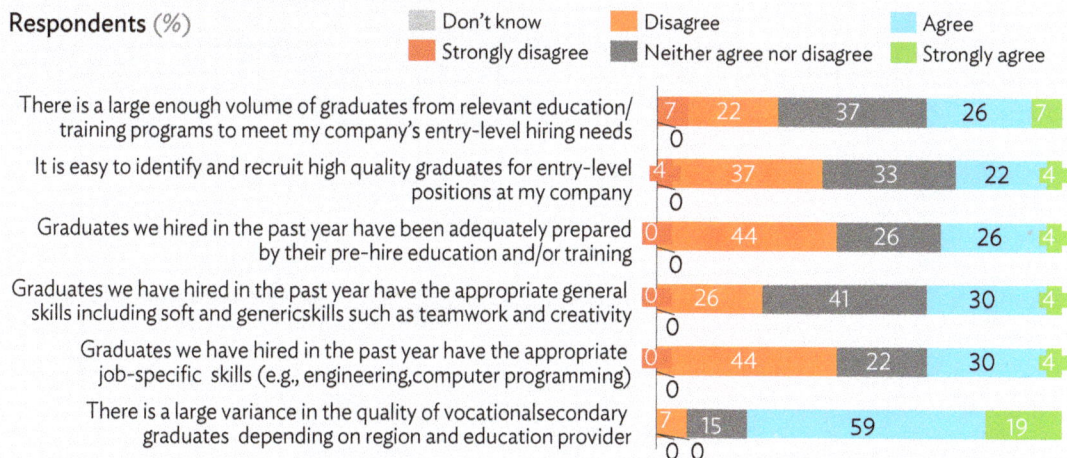

There is a large enough volume of graduates from relevant education/training programs to meet my company's entry-level hiring needs	7	22	37	26	7
	0				
It is easy to identify and recruit high quality graduates for entry-level positions at my company	4	37	33	22	4
	0				
Graduates we hired in the past year have been adequately prepared by their pre-hire education and/or training	0	44	26	26	4
	0				
Graduates we have hired in the past year have the appropriate general skills including soft and generic skills such as teamwork and creativity	0	26	41	30	4
	0				
Graduates we have hired in the past year have the appropriate job-specific skills (e.g., engineering, computer programming)	0	44	22	30	4
	0				
There is a large variance in the quality of vocational secondary graduates depending on region and education provider	7	15	59	19	
	0	0			

Source: Employer survey on impact of the Fourth Industrial Revolution on the automotive industry in Indonesia, n=40.

CHAPTER 2
Overview of the Training Landscape

This chapter provides insights into the performance of the technical and vocational education and training (TVET) industry in Indonesia as it prepares to deal with the challenges emerging from 4IR technology adoption. The insights are drawn from a survey of training institutions in Indonesia, complemented with insights from the employer surveys discussed in Chapter 1.

Encouragingly, there seem to be frequent updates of curricula and high reported levels of engagement with businesses. Of the training institutions surveyed, 45% said they communicate and coordinate with employers in relevant industries several times a year, and 23% said they engage on a monthly basis.

However, some gaps remain. Of the training institutions, 33% face difficulties filling student spots and vacancies across their courses; 4% even experience extreme difficulties in doing so. The key reasons for these difficulties appear to be related to the inability of trainees to differentiate among quality programs and students thinking training is not needed to find jobs. For example, 29% of the insitutions that have difficulty filling vacancies believe that trainees cannot distinguish the quality among programs and institutions, resulting in low uptake. Training institutions suggested some possible policy interventions that could address this. For example, 75% of training institutions cited government inspection and certification processes that assess quality of education institutions to be particularly impactful.

To better understand the supply of talent and skills for the adoption of 4IR technology, a survey of training institutions was commissioned in Indonesia, which included 44 institutions. The survey focused predominantly on TVET institutions of various levels of schooling. The sample was evenly split between private and public TVET institutions across different levels of education (Kinder–12, training institutions, and higher education); 33% of the funding from the surveyed institutions originates from public sources. Institutions of different sizes were sampled with a very even distribution: 25% train 10–100 students annually; 21%, 100–200; 23%, 200–1,000; and 23%, 1,000–10,000. The institutions offer courses across a wide range of industries with the largest share offering courses in education (32%) and hotel and tourism (20%).

Industry 4.0 Readiness

The majority of institutions feel well prepared for 4IR; however, many are requesting for additional technical and financial support (Figure 22). For example, 96% of institutions believe they have a good understanding of the skills needed to be developed to prepare graduates for their professional lives alongside 4IR technologies. Furthermore, 68% of institutions claim to already have dedicated programs related to 4IR skills, with 90% planning to develop or expand such programs by 2025. While 86% of institutions agree or strongly agree they will be able to adequately prepare their graduates as per their ongoing plans, 90% also agree or strongly agree with the statement that they needed additional technical and financial support, specifically for dealing with 4IR skill training.

Figure 22: Indonesian Training Institutions' Perception of their Readiness for 4IR

Training Sector: 4IR readiness

The majority of training institutions generally feel well equipped for 4IR, however 90% will require some additional support.

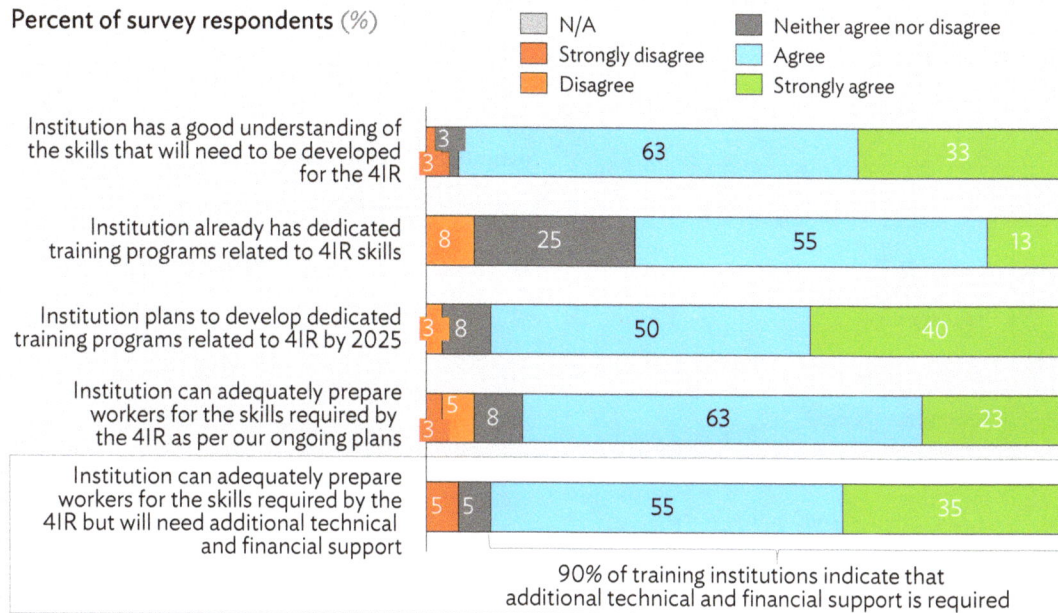

Percent of survey respondents (%)

Legend:
- N/A
- Strongly disagree
- Disagree
- Neither agree nor disagree
- Agree
- Strongly agree

Statement	Disagree/Strongly disagree	Neither	Agree	Strongly agree
Institution has a good understanding of the skills that will need to be developed for the 4IR	3 / 3		63	33
Institution already has dedicated training programs related to 4IR skills	8	25	55	13
Institution plans to develop dedicated training programs related to 4IR by 2025	3	8	50	40
Institution can adequately prepare workers for the skills required by the 4IR as per our ongoing plans	5 / 3	8	63	23
Institution can adequately prepare workers for the skills required by the 4IR but will need additional technical and financial support	5	5	55	35

90% of training institutions indicate that additional technical and financial support is required

4IF = Industry 4.0 or Fourth Industrial Revolution, N/A = not available.

Source: Training institution survey on impact of 4IR in Indonesia; n=40.

There seems to be somewhat limited alignment between the perceptions of training institutions and employers on skills that will be important for 4IR in the F&B manufacturing and automotive industries (Figure 23). The skill category most training institutions deem to become much more important over the next 5 years due to 4IR is complex problem-solving skills. This is closely followed by digital or information and communications technology (ICT); management; evaluation, judgment, and decision-making; and computer literacy skills. While employers agree on these skills for the most part, employers in the F&B manufacturing industry place far greater importance on digital/ICT and computer literacy skills. However, training institutions, as opposed to employers, believe a broader range of skills will gain importance, including communication and numeracy. Less than 5% of employers believe these skills to become much more important because of 4IR.

Curriculum

Aligning curricula with actual industry needs is one of the most important, but often most challenging components of an effective training and education industry. It relies on frequent updating and close communication with industry, given the speed of change in 4IR technologies in the workplace. Therefore, regular curriculum reviews are critical to keep pace with the skill changes related to 4IR. Most training

Figure 23: Potential Impact of 4IR on Importance of Different Skills in Indonesia over the Next 5 Years

Training Sector: 4IR readiness

Training institutions, as opposed to employers, believe a broader range of skills will gain importance, including communication and numeracy.

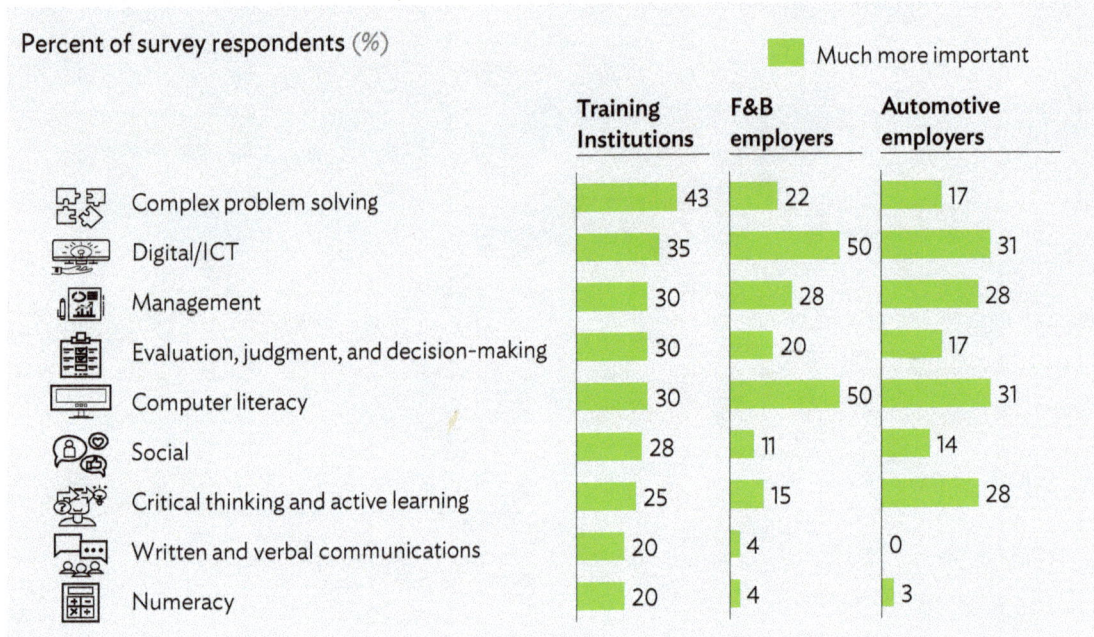

Percent of survey respondents (%)   ☐ Much more important

Skill	Training Institutions	F&B employers	Automotive employers
Complex problem solving	43	22	17
Digital/ICT	35	50	31
Management	30	28	28
Evaluation, judgment, and decision-making	30	20	17
Computer literacy	30	50	31
Social	28	11	14
Critical thinking and active learning	25	15	28
Written and verbal communications	20	4	0
Numeracy	20	4	3

4IR = Industry 4.0 or Fourth Industrial Revolution, F&B = food and beverage, ICT = information and communication technology.

Sources: Training institution survey on impact of 4IR in Indonesia, n=40; Employer survey on impact of 4IR on the F&B industry in Indonesia, n=46; Employer survey on impact of 4IR on the automotive industry in Indonesia, n=41.

institutions realize this and are placing a strong emphasis on curricula review. Of training institutions surveyed, 72% review and update their curricula annually (Figure 24).

Another aspect to consider is the content of the curriculum. Evidence from Indonesia suggests that on-the-job training and hands-on learning are two of the top three most effective instructional techniques according to vocational students.[21] Countries such as Denmark, Finland, France, Germany, Norway, and Switzerland spend 50%–75% of instructional time at the upper secondary level on practical or on-site training.[22] Though less focus is given to workplace-based training compared to leading international vocational programs, the results from Indonesia are nonetheless encouraging: 41% of time spent during training is workplace-based and an additional 33% on classroom-based student projects with less than a third of time allocated to theoretical work (Figure 25).

---

[21]   Asia Philanthropy Circle. 2017. *Catalysing Productive Livelihood: A Guide to Education Interventions with an Accelerated Path to Scale and Impact.* https://www.edumap-indonesia.asiaphilanthropycircle.org/.

[22]   OECD. 2010. *Learning for Jobs : The OECD International Survey of VET Systems: First Results and Technical Report.* http://www.oecd.org/education/skills-beyond-school/Learning%20for%20Jobs%20book.pdf.

Figure 24: The Frequency in which Indonesian Training Institutions Review and Update Curricula

Seventy-two percent of all training institutions review and update their curricula annually.

Percent of survey respondents (%)

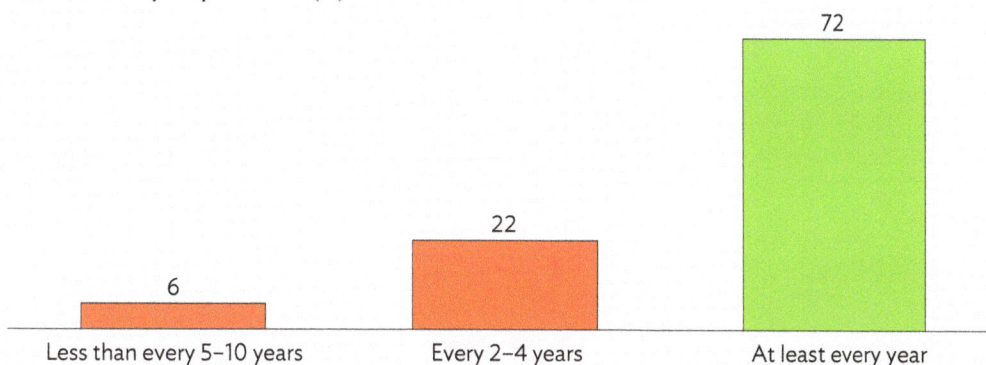

Source: Training institution survey on impact of the Fourth Industrial Revolution in Indonesia; n=32.

Figure 25: Time Devoted to Different Types of Training In TVET Institutions in Indonesia

Though lower compared to leading international vocational programs, Indonesia's focus on workplace-based training is encouraging.

Average percentage share of total time spent on training type at surveyed institutions (%)

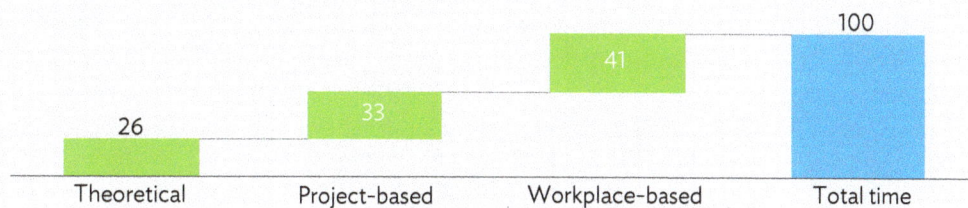

According to OECD research, more than three-quarters of vocational training program in Denmark, Finland, France, Germany, Norway, and Switzerland at the upper secondary level spend 50%–75% of instructional time in practical or on-site training.

OECD = Organisation for Economic Co-operation and Development, TVET = technical and vocational education and training.

Note: Theoretical training refers to lectures, Project-based refers to student projects, and Workplace-based refers to on-the-job training such as industry apprenticeships.

Source: Training institution survey on impact of the Fourth Industrial Revolution in Indonesia; n=32; M. Kuczera. 2010. *Learning for Jobs - The OECD International Survey of VET Systems: First Results and Technical Report.*

Figure 26: Prevalence of Technology-Related Courses and Technology-Based Delivery in Teaching at Training Institutions in Indonesia

Training Sector: Curriculum

Training institutions provide courses to teach 4IR relevant skills and technologies, but the uptake of 4IR in the classroom is largely limited.

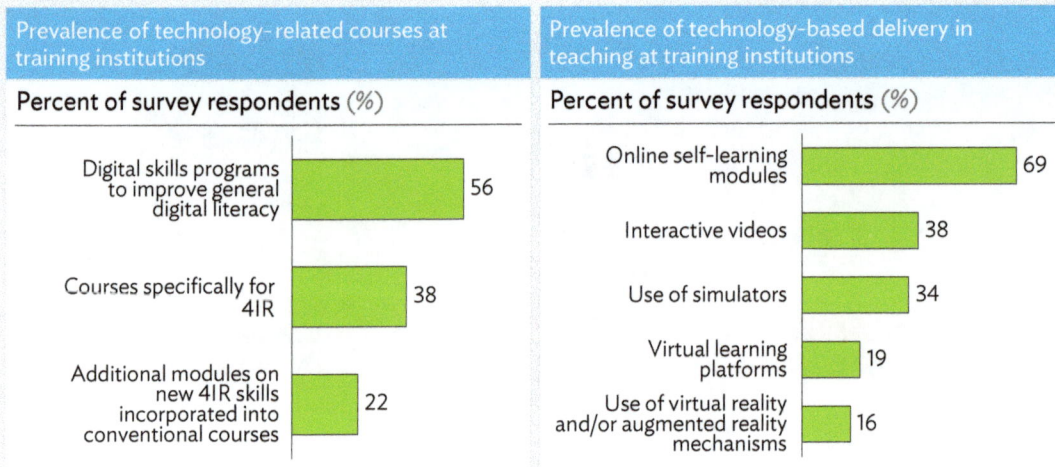

Prevalence of technology-related courses at training institutions	Prevalence of technology-based delivery in teaching at training institutions

Percent of survey respondents (%)

Digital skills programs to improve general digital literacy	56
Courses specifically for 4IR	38
Additional modules on new 4IR skills incorporated into conventional courses	22

Percent of survey respondents (%)

Online self-learning modules	69
Interactive videos	38
Use of simulators	34
Virtual learning platforms	19
Use of virtual reality and/or augmented reality mechanisms	16

4IR = Industry 4.0 or Fourth Industrial Revolution.

Source: Training institution survey on impact of 4IR in Indonesia; n=32.

While training institutions surveyed in Indonesia provide courses relevant for 4IR, the adoption of 4IR technologies in the classroom is mixed (Figure 26). Of training institutions surveyed, 56% run digital programs at improving digital literacy, 38% said they rolled out courses specifically focusing on 4IR, and 22% incorporated additional modules on 4IR-relevant skills into their conventional courses. On technology adoption in the classroom, some technologies are heavily favored. Already 69% of institutions make use of online self-learning tools, but only 38% use interactive videos, 34% employ some form of simulators for technical training, 19% adopted virtual learning platforms, and only 16% of training institutions use virtual or augmented reality. Since the latter technologies are more nascent and expensive, the limited uptake is likely linked to a lack of information about the latest applications and/or financial constraints.

Many training institutions also engage in a range of programs and activities in addition to training courses that are aimed at providing students with better information and access to career opportunities and support (Figure 27). For example, on the career front, 78% of institutions surveyed arrange meetings with career coaches for advice and 63% arrange visits and field trips to companies. About half of institutions surveyed help with curriculum vitae preparation or arrange for company representatives to visit the institutions.

But there is room for improvement as less than 40% of institutions provide scholarships for students from low-income backgrounds, as well as interview support. Only 28% say they provide noncareer advice to students, such as counseling on personal or financial matters.

Figure 27: Programs Provided in Addition to Training Courses in Indonesia

Training Sector: Curriculum

In addition to training courses, a number of training institutions provide programs such as career advice and company visits.

Percent of survey respondents (%)

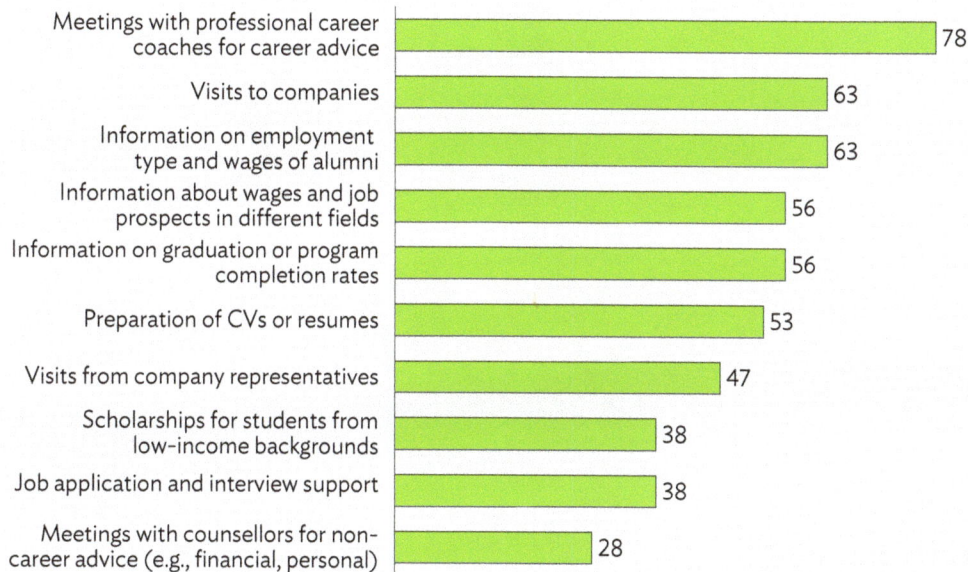

Program	%
Meetings with professional career coaches for career advice	78
Visits to companies	63
Information on employment type and wages of alumni	63
Information about wages and job prospects in different fields	56
Information on graduation or program completion rates	56
Preparation of CVs or resumes	53
Visits from company representatives	47
Scholarships for students from low-income backgrounds	38
Job application and interview support	38
Meetings with counsellors for non-career advice (e.g., financial, personal)	28

CV = curriculum vitae.

Source: Training institution survey on impact of the Fourth Industrial Revolution in Indonesia; n=32.

Industry Engagement

Training institutions surveyed displayed very positive levels of interaction with potential employers, in contrast to anecdotal evidence from targeted interviews with training institutions and from in-country consultation workshops. Of training institutions, 45% said they communicate and coordinate with employers in relevant industries several times a year and 23% said they engage on a monthly basis (Figure 28).

Of training institutions surveyed, 84% work with employers on train-the-teacher programs to foster industry relevance. About 77% indicate they organize apprenticeships or gather input for the curriculum from the industry. (Figure 29).

In addition, 61% work with industry to provide teaching placement and 58% work with employers to organize job fairs and 55% use employer provided equipment, facilities, or technology for hands-on training. Still more than half are able to organize workplace-based training for their students.

Figure 28: Frequency of Training Institutions' Communication with Employers in Indonesia

Training Sector: Employers

Ninety-one percent of training institutions communicate with employers at least 2 times a year.

Percent of survey respondents[a] (%)

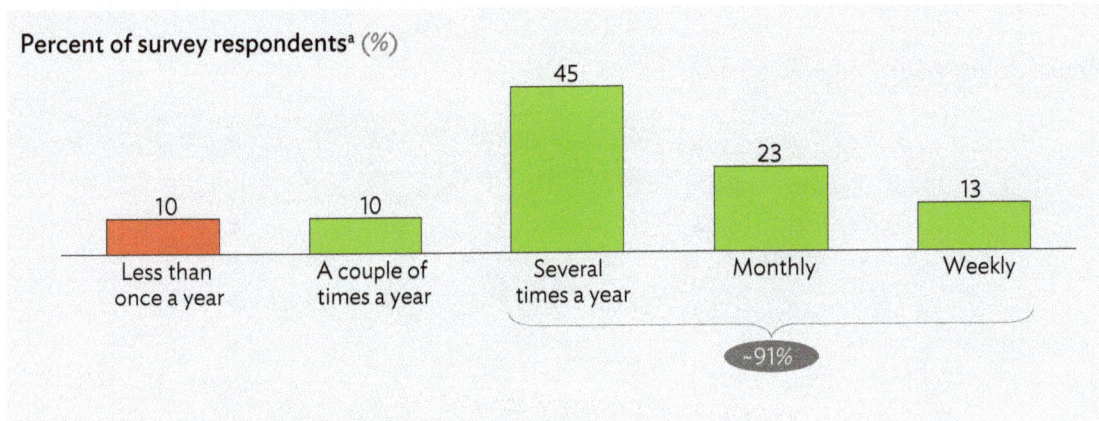

a   May not add up to 100% due to rounding.

Source: Training institution survey on impact of the Fourth Industrial Revolution in Indonesia; n=31.

Figure 29: Potential Partnerships and Engagement Between Industry and Training Institutions in Indonesia

Training Sector: Employers

Training institutions in Indonesia report active engagement with employers on train-the-teacher programs being most common.

Percent of surveyed training institutions (%)

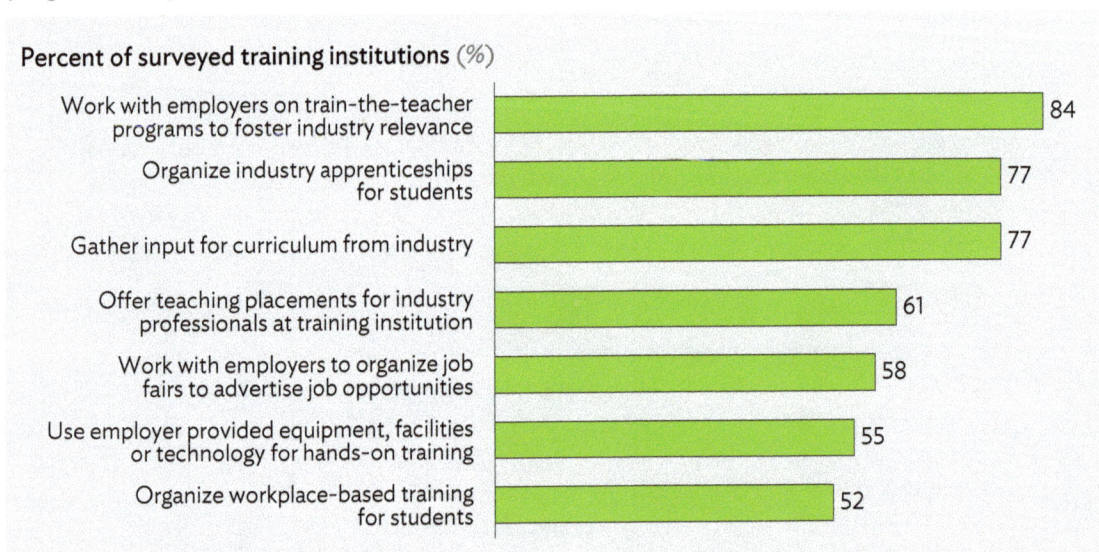

Work with employers on train-the-teacher programs to foster industry relevance	84
Organize industry apprenticeships for students	77
Gather input for curriculum from industry	77
Offer teaching placements for industry professionals at training institution	61
Work with employers to organize job fairs to advertise job opportunities	58
Use employer provided equipment, facilities or technology for hands-on training	55
Organize workplace-based training for students	52

Source: Training institution survey on impact of the Fourth Industrial Revolution in Indonesia; n=31.

These levels of engagements are similar to findings from employers' surveys. While potentially not representative of general employer activity across the all industries, the F&B manufacturing and automotive industries are still important employers (Figure 30). On average, the automotive manufacturing industry appears to be more active in engaging educators beyond offering input on the curriculum and industry apprenticeships to students. For example, 74% of employers in the automotive manufacturing industry claim to provide equipment and training opportunities for educators.

Over 56% of F&B manufacturing employers and 68% of automotive employers surveyed agree or strongly agree with the statement that most of their staff have received training in the past 12 months. For F&B employers, 68% and 75% for automotive employers claim to heavily invest in training internally. The amount of training received differs by occupation. For example, administrative and customer-facing workers appear to receive less training regardless of industry (Figure 31). The type of training received also varies by occupation. While, on average workers receive more days of on-the-job training versus formal professional training, the ratio of on-the-job to formal training is higher for lower-skilled jobs, such as administrative and manual jobs. In the automotive manufacturing industry, one reason for the lack of formal training could be that employers claim to have difficulty finding quality training providers. Only a quarter of employers agreed or strongly agreed with the statement that they are able to find training providers.

Figure 30: Potential Partnerships and Engagement Between Industry and Training Institutions in the Food and Beverage and Automotive Industries in Indonesia

Training Sector: Employers

On average, the automotive industry appears to be more active in engaging teaching institutions outside of apprenticeships and curriculum.

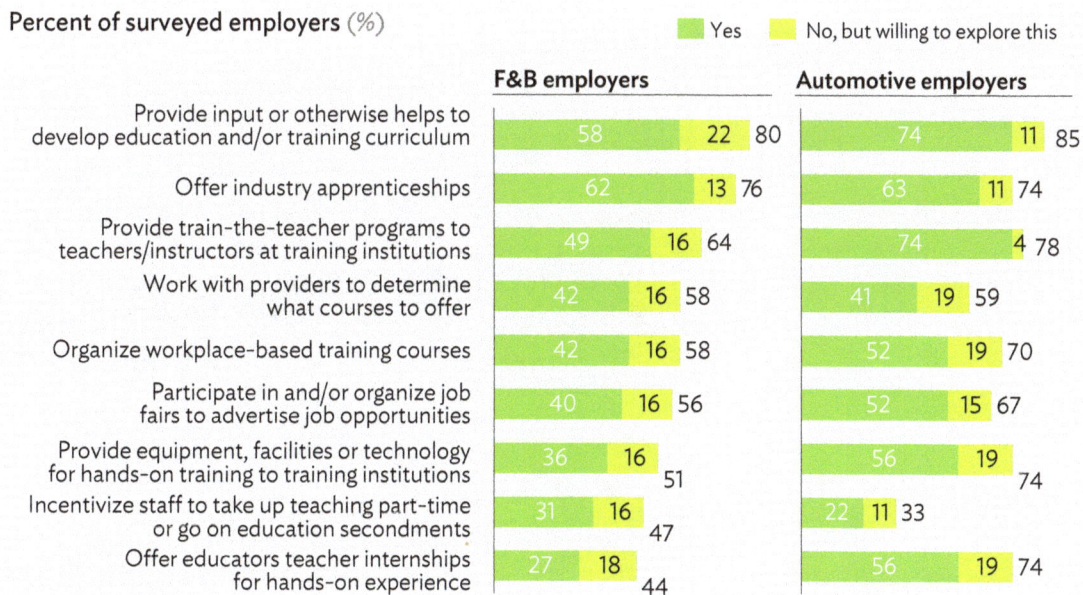

Percent of surveyed employers (%)   ■ Yes   ■ No, but willing to explore this

	F&B employers			Automotive employers		
Provide input or otherwise helps to develop education and/or training curriculum	58	22	80	74	11	85
Offer industry apprenticeships	62	13	76	63	11	74
Provide train-the-teacher programs to teachers/instructors at training institutions	49	16	64	74	4	78
Work with providers to determine what courses to offer	42	16	58	41	19	59
Organize workplace-based training courses	42	16	58	52	19	70
Participate in and/or organize job fairs to advertise job opportunities	40	16	56	52	15	67
Provide equipment, facilities or technology for hands-on training to training institutions	36	16	51	56	19	74
Incentivize staff to take up teaching part-time or go on education secondments	31	16	47	22	11	33
Offer educators teacher internships for hands-on experience	27	18	44	56	19	74

F&B = food and beverage.

Source: Employer survey on impact of the Fourth Industrial Revolution on the F&B industry in Indonesia, n=45; Employer survey on impact of the Fourth Industrial Revolution on the automotive industry in Indonesia, n=27.

Figure 31: Current Annual Training while in Employment in Indonesia's Food and Beverage and Automotive Industries, by Training Channel

Training Sector: Employers

On average, workers in the automotive industry receive similar amounts of training to those in the F&B industry.

Training required by channel, days per year

Type of training | ▇ On-the-Job ▇ Formal mid-career

Occupation	F&B industry		Automotive industry	
	On-the-Job	Formal	On-the-Job	Formal
Managerial	6	5	7	5
Administrative	4	2	6	3
Technical	6	5	8	6
Manual job	7	3	8	4
Customer-facing	4	3	6	3

F&B = food and beverage.

Source: Employer survey on impact of the Fourth Industrial Revolution on the F&B industry in Indonesia, n=40; Employer survey on impact of the Fourth Industrial Revolution on the automotive industry in Indonesia, n=41.

Teachers, Trainers, and Instructors

It is encouraging that many training institutions are actively engaged in performance assessment and professional development of their teaching and training staff: 81% give formal annual or semiannual performance reviews or provide frequent feedback (Figure 32); 55% allow instructors to devote time during working hours to pursue avenues to refresh their practical knowledge and/or learn new techniques on their own; and 77% provide ongoing professional development and industry-relevant training (e.g., industry seminars and industry exposure) for instructors.

Performance and Policy Support

Of the surveyed training institutions, 33% face difficulties filling student vacancies across their courses (Figure 33); 4% even experience extreme difficulties in doing so. The key reasons for these difficulties appear to be related to the inability of trainees to differentiate quality programs and students thinking that training is not needed to find jobs. For example, 29% of the institutions facing difficulties filling

Figure 32: Practices in Trainer Performance Assessment and Professional Development in Indonesia

Training Sector: Instructors

On average, training institutions focus more on instructor and teacher assessment than professional development.

Percent of survey respondents (%)

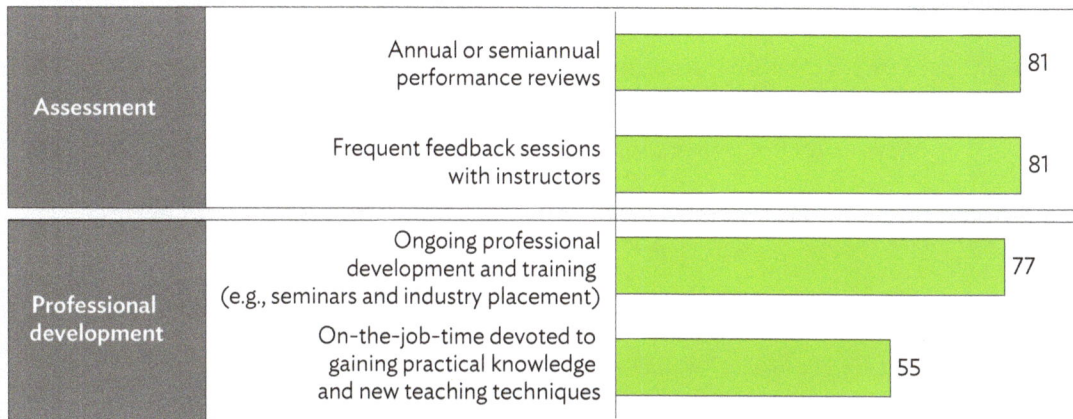

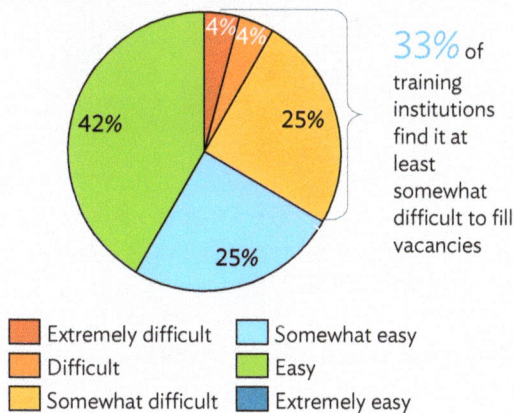

Assessment	Annual or semiannual performance reviews	81
	Frequent feedback sessions with instructors	81
Professional development	Ongoing professional development and training (e.g., seminars and industry placement)	77
	On-the-job-time devoted to gaining practical knowledge and new teaching techniques	55

Source: Training institution survey on impact of the Fourth Industrial Revolution in Indonesia; n=31.

Figure 33: Difficulty in Filling Student Vacancies in Training Institutions in Indonesia

Training Sector: Policy

Thirty-three percent of training institutions find it difficult to fill vacancies, some as a result of students failing to differentiate quality programs.

Percent of survey respondents (%)

4% 4% 42% 25% 25%

33% of training institutions find it at least somewhat difficult to fill vacancies

- Extremely difficult
- Difficult
- Somewhat difficult
- Somewhat easy
- Easy
- Extremely easy

Why is it difficult to fill seats at your institution?
Percent of survey respondents with difficulties (%)

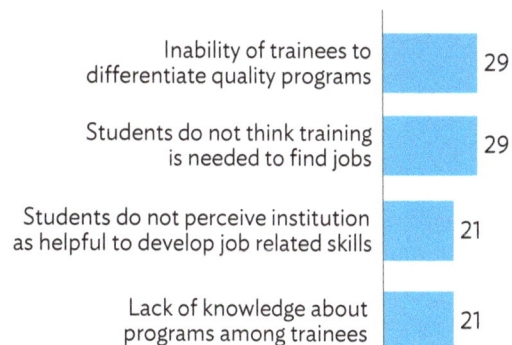

Inability of trainees to differentiate quality programs	29
Students do not think training is needed to find jobs	29
Students do not perceive institution as helpful to develop job related skills	21
Lack of knowledge about programs among trainees	21

Source: Training institution survey on impact of the Fourth Industrial Revolution in Indonesia; n=24.

Figure 34: Training Institutions' Perception of Policy Effectiveness in Indonesia

Training Sector: Policy

Policy aimed at quality assessment of institutions is deemed as having the most positive impact by training institutions

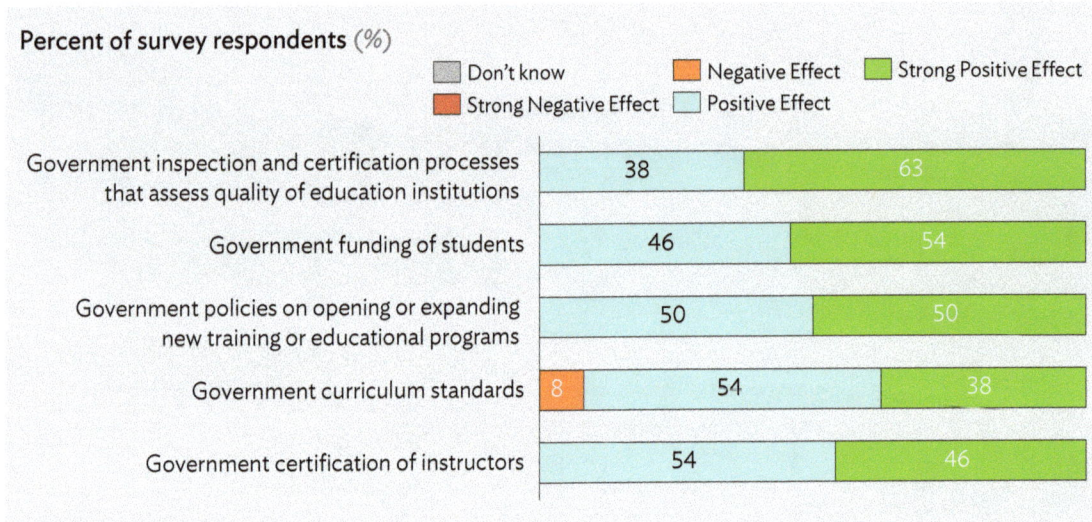

Percent of survey respondents (%)

Legend: Don't know | Negative Effect | Strong Positive Effect | Strong Negative Effect | Positive Effect

Category	Values
Government inspection and certification processes that assess quality of education institutions	38 / 63
Government funding of students	46 / 54
Government policies on opening or expanding new training or educational programs	50 / 50
Government curriculum standards	8 / 54 / 38
Government certification of instructors	54 / 46

Source: Training institution survey on impact of the Fourth Industrial Revolution in Indonesia; n=24.

vacancies believe an inability among trainees to differentiate programs and institutions by quality to be responsible for the low uptake, and 29% believe students do not perceive training is needed to find jobs.

Training institutions are looking to policy to address some of these challenges. Across all of the areas surveyed, training institutions reported that government policy interventions were having positive effects (Figure 34). However, it is clear more are needed. For example, 75% of training institutions cited government inspection and certification processes that assess quality of education institutions to have a particularly great impact (Figure 35). This finding appears consistent with the earlier results that training institutions believe students lack information on the quality of different training providers.

Supply and Demand Mismatches

According to the training institutions surveyed, the most common reason graduates may not be able to find a job is the certifications provided are not well-recognized by employers (Figure 36). The second most common reason is graduates are not adequately prepared for jobs they are looking for.

Another area of mismatch between industry and training institutions is in the actual skills or level of skills (i.e., basic, intermediate, advanced) graduates possess when they finish training or education. There seems to be a big misalignment between training institutions' expectations of graduate preparedness for work, and employers' expectations about graduates' skills required to perform well in entry-level roles, as well as their general and job-specific skills (Figure 37).

Figure 35: Training Institutions' Perspective on Public Policies with Greatest Impact on Training Provision

Training Sector: Policy

Training institutions believe that quality assurance mechanisms would be the most helpful policy.

Percent of survey respondents (%)

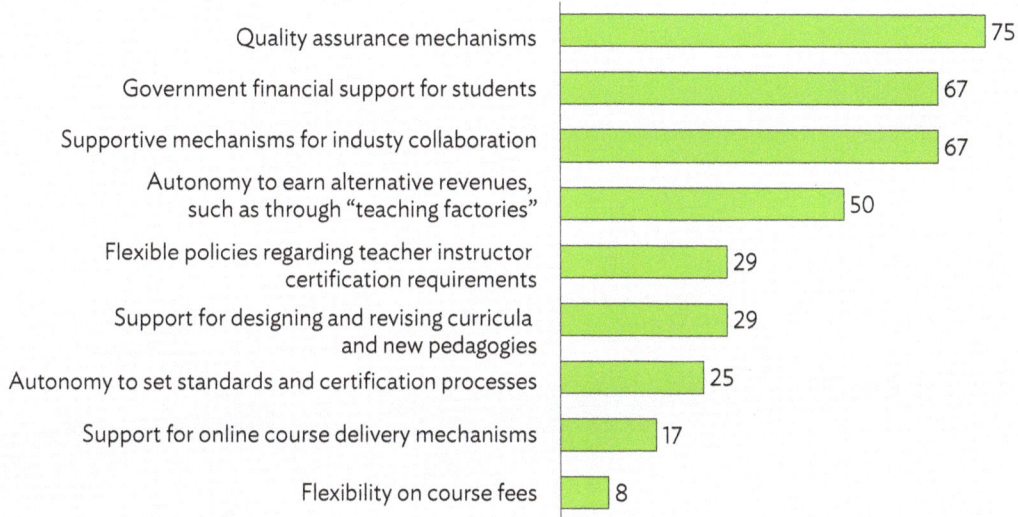

Policy	%
Quality assurance mechanisms	75
Government financial support for students	67
Supportive mechanisms for industy collaboration	67
Autonomy to earn alternative revenues, such as through "teaching factories"	50
Flexible policies regarding teacher instructor certification requirements	29
Support for designing and revising curricula and new pedagogies	29
Autonomy to set standards and certification processes	25
Support for online course delivery mechanisms	17
Flexibility on course fees	8

Source: Training institution survey on impact of the Fourth Industrial Revolution in Indonesia; n=24.

Figure 36: Reasons Students are Unable to find Employment after Graduation in Indonesia

Training Sector: Students

Training institutions believe a lack of certification recognition and of preparation for jobs by training programs are key employment barriers.

Ranking score, 1–Most common; 5–Least common

Rank		Average Ranking
1	Graduates' certifications are not well-recognized by employers	1.81
2	Education and training programs do not adequately prepare job seekers for job opportunities	2.66
3	Enough jobs, but students unaware of job opportunities	3.22
4	Not enough opportunities for job seekers to complete relevant education or training for job opportunities	3.38
5	Not enough job opportunities	3.94

Source: Training institution survey on impact of the Fourth Industrial Revolution in Indonesia; n=32.

This significant mismatch in skill expectations between employers and training institutions is surprising given the high reported levels of engagement between employers and training institutions, as noted earlier. These results suggest that while training institutions may have a good understanding of the skill categories of rising importance for 4IR, the actual implementation of skill training, or depth and specific type of skills taught do not match industry requirements.

Figure 37: Perceptions of Graduates' Preparedness for Entry-Level Positions in Indonesia

Training Sector: Students

On average, training institutions are much more optimistic about the preparedness of graduates for work than what employers report.

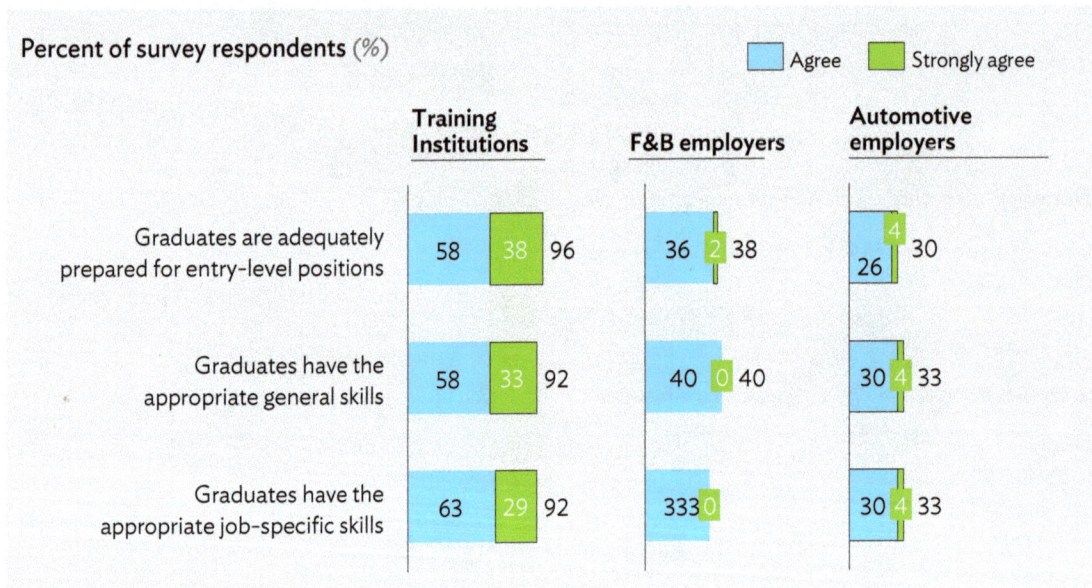

Percent of survey respondents (%)

Agree   Strongly agree

	Training Institutions	F&B employers	Automotive employers
Graduates are adequately prepared for entry-level positions	58 / 38 / 96	36 / 2 / 38	26 / 4 / 30
Graduates have the appropriate general skills	58 / 33 / 92	40 / 0 / 40	30 / 4 / 33
Graduates have the appropriate job-specific skills	63 / 29 / 92	33 / 3 / 0	30 / 4 / 33

F&B = food and beverage.

Source: Training institution survey on impact of the Fourth Industrial Revolution (4IR) in Indonesia, n=24; Employer survey on impact of 4IR on the F&B industry in Indonesia, n=45; Employer survey on impact of 4IR on the automotive industry in Indonesia, n=27.

CHAPTER 3
National Policy Responses

A thorough scan of all ongoing policies and programs by the government, industry, and civil society in Indonesia reveals a range of strategies that seek to improve the readiness of the national workforce for Industry 4.0 (4IR). Particularly with the recent development of the Making Indonesia 4.0 strategy, much focus is placed on stimulating higher technology adoption by firms, fostering government–industry–civil society collaboration for training frameworks, and creating more flexible pathways for skills development. However, more limited focus is demonstrated in the areas of building awareness of in-demand jobs and skills for 4IR, creating incentives for skills development, establishing lifelong learning models, ensuring the relevance and agility of education and training curriculums to emerging skill needs, developing inclusive models, and social protection mechanisms for the emerging class of gig economy workers. The country's implementation strategy is also relatively robust, with a clearly articulated vision for 4IR, specific targets based on global trends and local data. However, this study observed that integration with the country's employment and skills strategy, coordination across relevant government departments, industry–institution alignment, and incentives for stakeholders to ensure high quality training and education systems are limited.

Overview of Industry 4.0 Policy Landscape

4IR is an important part of Indonesia's policy agenda to achieve its goal of becoming 1 of the 10 largest economies in terms of gross domestic product globally by 2030.[23] The Government of Indonesia commissioned a study in 2018 to understand the country's 4IR readiness in comparison with other countries, and developed a strategy, Making Indonesia 4.0, to implement 4IR.[24]

Led by the Ministry of Industry (MOI), this strategy outlines the country's implementation road map for 4IR. It shortlists five priority industries (F&B, automotive, textiles and apparel, chemicals, and electronics) based on their assessed potential benefit from 4IR and implementation feasibility (footnote 23). The strategy details action plans for each industry based on 10 outlined priorities, which include building national digital infrastructure, attracting foreign investment for technology transfer, boosting the quality of local human resources, designing incentives for technology investments, and harmonizing regulations and policies (footnote 23).

---

[23] Indonesia Investments. 2018. Widodo Launches Road map for Industry 4.0: "Making Indonesia 4.0." *Indonesia Investments Business Columns.* https://www.indonesia-investments.com/business/business-columns/widodo-launches-roadmap-for-industry-4.0-making-indonesia-4.0/item8711.

[24] Ministry of Industry of Republic of Indonesia. 2018. *Making Indonesia 4.0.* http://www.kemenperin.go.id/kebijakan-industri.

Besides this strategy, the following national policy documents reflect 4IR elements. Though not specifically articulated as 4IR, these mention new technology adoption and the consequent need for workforce skills preparedness:

(i)   **Presidential Decree No. 9 Year 2016 on "Revitalizing SMKs to Improve the Quality and Competitiveness of Indonesian Human Resources."** To improve the industry relevance of vocational education and employability of graduates, the government introduced the concept of demand-driven curricula to vocational senior high schools through this decree.[25]

(ii)   **Policy Road map on Vocational Education 2017–2025.** Developed by the Coordinating Ministry of Economic Affairs (CMEA) in consultation with the Ministry of Education and Culture (MENC); and the Ministry of Research and Technology (MORT), this document sets out the guidelines for how vocational schools and curriculums should be run.[26] These guidelines include the minimum level of teaching equipment that should be present in institutions, and the standardization of curricular content for each educational level.

(iii) **National Medium-Term Industrial Development Plan 2015–2019.** This refers to the country's 5-year medium-term economic development road map, which includes a strategy to increase the number of education and training institutions to enhance the quality of human resources.[27] Emphasis is placed on developing a competency or skill-based workforce.

(iv)   **National Industrial Development Master Plan 2015–2035.** This outlines the country's 20-year long-term economic strategy, which focuses on the development of human resources by facilitating competency testing, human resources certifications, and a national set of work competency standards (*Standard Kompetensi Kerja Nasional Indonesia* or SKKNI) for industry.[28]

(v)   **Manpower Regulation No. 36/2016 and the "National Apprenticeship Framework Program."** Led by the Ministry of Manpower (MOM), this regulation forms the legal framework for employers to implement apprenticeship programs in the country (footnote 27).[29] As part of this, the MOM establishes skills development centers across Indonesia to provide individuals seeking jobs with opportunities for training, job matching and placement, as well as career counseling.

(vi)   **"Community BLK Cooperation" Plan (**Kerja Sama BLK Komunitas**).** Spearheaded by a collaboration between the MOM and the MENC, this plan seeks to expand training access across the country by strengthening the capacities of upper secondary schools (SMKs) and vocational training centers (*Balai Latihan Kerja* or BLK).[30] Selected recipient institutions will receive assistance for the development of new workshop buildings, provision of training equipment, and implementation of new training courses for students and training programs for instructors.

---

[25]   Sekretariat Kabinet Republik Indonesia. 2016. *Presidential Decree No. 9 Year 2016 on "Revitalizing SMKs to Improve the Quality and Competitiveness of Indonesian Human Resources."* https://kemdikbud.go.id/main/files/download/e451d9ec3a04121.

[26]   International NGO Forum on Indonesian Development. 2017. *Vokasi di Era Revolusi Industri.* https://workequal.org/storage/app/uploads/public/5b7/fbb/d70/5b7fbbd7055d9469489896.pdf.

[27]   Government of Indonesia, Ministry of Industry. 2010. *National Medium-Term Industrial Development Plan 2015–2019.* http://www.kemenperin.go.id/profil/71/rencana-strategis-kementerian-perindustrian.

[28]   Government of Indonesia, Ministry of Industry. 2015. *National industrial Development Master Plan 2015–2035.* https://kemenperin.go.id/ripin.pdf.

[29]   ILO. 2018. *Improving Practical Skills of Job Seekers through Apprenticeship.* https://www.ilo.org/jakarta/info/public/pr/WCMS_636126/lang--en/index.htm.

[30]   Government of Indonesia, Ministry of Manpower. 2019. *Penandatanganan Kerja Sama "BLK" Komunitas Tahap I Tahun 2019 antara Kementerian Ketenagakerjaan dengan Lembaga Penerima Bantuan* https://www.kemenkumham.go.id/publikasi/siaran-pers/penandatanganan-kerja-sama-"BLK"-komunitas-tahap-i-tahun-2019-antara-kementerian-ketenagakerjaan-dengan-lembaga-penerima-bantuan.

(vii) **Ministry of Research and Technology (MORT) Strategy 2015–2019.** This focuses on improving the access, relevance, and quality of higher education for human resource development to meet industry needs.[31]

(viii) **National Medium-Term Development Plan 2020–2024** (in progress). This places a strong focus on the role of higher education to support technological change, innovation, and entrepreneurship.[32] In response to this, the MENC is currently preparing a medium-term investment plan for higher education which will aim to accelerate innovations in new technology and stimulate entrepreneurship in the country's top universities, while also developing advanced skills in regional universities.

Table 1 summarizes some of Indonesia's key policy documents relating to 4IR.

Table 1: Key Policies Relevant to Managing the Impact of 4IR on Skills in Indonesia

Policy Document	Responsible entity	Relevance
Making Indonesia 4.0	Ministry of Industry	Outlines the country's 4IR implementation road map, with five priority industries and 10 priorities shortlisted
Presidential Decree No. 9 Year 2016 on "Revitalizing SMKs to Improve the Quality and Competitiveness of Indonesian Human Resources"	Ministry of Education and Culture	Introduced demand-driven curricula to vocational senior high schools
Manpower Regulation No. 36/2016 and the National Apprenticeship Framework Program	Ministry of Manpower	Legal framework for companies to implement apprenticeship programs for students
Community BLK Cooperation	Ministry of Education and Culture	Expand training access by strengthening SMK and BLK capacities

4IR = Industry 4.0 or Fourth Industrial Revolution, BLK = *Balai Latihan Kerja* or vocational training center, SMK = upper secondary school (English equivalent of a Bahasa Indonesia term).

Sources: Government of Indonesia, Ministry of Industry. 2018. *Making Indonesia 4.0.* http://www.kemenperin.go.id/kebijakan-industri; Sekretariat Kabinet Republik Indonesia. 2016. *Presidential Decree No. 9 Year 2016 on "Revitalizing SMKs to Improve the Quality and Competitiveness of Indonesian Human Resources."* https://kemdikbud.go.id/main/files/download/e451d9ec3a04121; ILO. 2018. *Improving Practical Skills of Job Seekers through Apprenticeship.* https://www.ilo.org/jakarta/info/public/pr/WCMS_636126/lang--en/index.htm; Government of Indonesia, Ministry of Manpower. 2019. *Penandatanganan Kerja Sama "BLK" Komunitas Tahap I Tahun 2019 antara Kementerian Ketenagakerjaan dengan Lembaga Penerima Bantuan* https://www.kemenkumham.go.id/publikasi/siaran-pers/penandatanganan-kerja-sama-"BLK"-komunitas-tahap-i-tahun-2019-antara-kementerian-ketenagakerjaan-dengan-lembaga-penerima-bantuan.

Assessment of Current Indonesian Policy Approaches Related to Industry 4.0

A diagnostic approach was taken to understand two important aspects of Indonesia's 4IR policy approach: (i) "the what" or the specific policies Indonesia adopts and how they compare to a set of international best practice approaches in preparing workers for 4IR; and (ii) "the how" or the implementation mechanisms supporting 4IR efforts in government.

---

[31]   Government of Indonesia, Ministry of Research, Technology, and Higher Education. 2019. *Policies and Programs.* https://international.ristekdikti.go.id/policies-and-programs/.

[32]   Based on consultations with stakeholders of the Government of Indonesia in July 2019.

Assessment of Policy Actions ("The What")

The country's policies and programs were grouped into nine action areas assessed to be most crucial to managing the impact of 4IR on jobs and skills.[33] Figure 38 shows the current degree of focus by the country for each action area. The current degree of focus on each action area was rated as "strong," "moderate," or "weak" based on the analyzed extent of the policies' coverage in scope and scale compared to those observed in international best practices.

Figure 38: Degree of Focus of Policy Actions to Manage the Impact of 4IR on Jobs and Skills in Indonesia

Degree of current focus: ■ Strong ■ Moderate ■ Weak

Action Agenda	Key Action	Assessment
Stimulate Industry 4.0 adoption and worker reskilling efforts	Ensure strong and even adoption of 4IR technology across firms and workers	Moderate
	Build awareness of in-demand jobs and skills, as well as the benefits and opportunities of training	Weak
	Incentivize employers and workers to participate in skills development	Weak
	Foster close collaboration between governments, industry, and civil society to create relevant and effective nationwide retraining frameworks	Moderate
Create new flexible qualification pathways	Establish effective lifelong learning models	Weak
	Ensure relevance and agility of education and training curriculums to emerging skill needs	Weak
	Encourage focus on skills rather than just qualifications in both recruitment and national labor market strategies	Moderate
Build inclusiveness to extend 4IR benefits to all workers	Build inclusive models that allow underserved groups to benefit from 4IR	Weak
	Create social protection mechanisms for workers taking on flexible forms of labor	Weak

4IR = Industry 4.0 or Fourth Industrial Revolution.

Note: Degree of focus was assessed based on the following criteria: "Strong" – few or no gaps between the country's coverage of policy actions and coverage seen in international best practices; "Moderate" – medium level of gaps between the country's coverage of policy actions and coverage seen in international best practices; and "Weak" – significant gaps between the country's coverage of policy actions and coverage seen in international best practices.

Source: Literature review; AlphaBeta analysis.

---

[33]   Based on AlphaBeta research on international best practices for policy actions that manage the impact of 4IR on jobs and skills. More details of these best practices are in Microsoft and AlphaBeta. 2019. *Preparing for AI: The Implications of Artificial Intelligence for Jobs and Skills in Asian Economies.* https://news.microsoft.com/apac/2019/08/26/preparing-for-ai-the-implications-of-artificial-intelligence-for-jobs-and-skills-in-asian-economies/.

Overall, the current degree of focus on the range of 4IR-relevant policy areas is relatively low in Indonesia. A moderate level of focus is placed on stimulating higher technology adoption by firms (through the Making Indonesia 4.0 strategy), fostering government–industry–civil society collaboration for training frameworks, and creating more flexible pathways for skills development. However, more limited focus is demonstrated in the areas of building awareness of in-demand jobs and skills for 4IR, creating incentives for skills development, establishing lifelong learning models, ensuring the relevance and agility of education and training curricula to emerging skill needs, developing inclusive models, and on social protection mechanisms for the emerging class of gig economy workers. More specifically:

(i) **Stimulating industry adoption and worker reskilling.** A global 4IR readiness assessment indicated that Indonesia was currently in the nascent phase, due to its relatively weak performance in four areas: human capital, level of technology adoption, openness to trade and digital infrastructure.[34] One particular challenge is in raising awareness of in-demand skills. In a recent survey to understand the attitudes of Indonesian employers and their workers toward reskilling for AI, the most commonly cited reason (59% of employers and 45% of workers) for not undergoing training courses was there was lack of time. Other key reasons include a lack of awareness of which courses to take (37% and 33%), and the opinion that there were no suitable training programs (43% and 23%).[35] These findings point toward a lack of awareness of the importance of reskilling and reskilling opportunities. To address this, the government is currently looking to implement a series of policies, including tax incentives for in-service worker training; assessment of in demand skills and a training list for them; and the establishment of a National Vocational Training Committee with a three-pronged strategy to skill, reskill, and upskill workers.[36] However, prior to their implementation, consultations with industry stakeholders reveal a general lack of understanding of the 4IR skills required across industries, as well as how workers may be trained in them. A further challenge in this area relates to providing incentives to employers and workers to engage in skill development. This was demonstrated to be linked to a strong reliance on short-term contracting in the labor market, leading to underinvestment in training by companies and the workers' lack of motivation (due to the absence of any foreseeable career progression) to invest in their own skills development.[37] Recent surveys also reveal that less than a quarter of Indonesian companies conduct formal in-house training for their workers, and 4% more employers would rather hire new staff with the required skills, as compared to those willing to retrain existing workers to attain these skills.[38] On a more positive note, there were significant efforts to strengthen the adoption of 4IR technologies by firms, and to foster closer collaboration between governments, industry, and civil society to create retraining frameworks.

34   World Bank and AT Kearney. 2018. *Readiness for the Future of Production Report 2018.* http://www3.weforum.org/docs/FOP_Readiness_Report_2018.pdf.

35   Microsoft and IDC. 2018. *Microsoft – IDC Study: Artificial Intelligence to Nearly Double the Rate of Innovation in Asia Pacific by 2021.* https://news.microsoft.com/apac/2019/02/20/microsoft-idc-study-artificial-intelligence-to-nearly-double-the-rate-of-innovation-in-asia-pacific-by-2021/.

36   Based on consultations with the CMEA, MOI, and MOM in July 2019.

37   E. Allen. 2016. Emma Allen – Raising Indonesian labor productivity. *Nikkei Asian Review.* https://asia.nikkei.com/Economy/Emma-Allen-Raising-Indonesian-labor-productivity.

38   World Economic Forum. 2018. *The Future of Jobs Report 2018.* Available at: http://www3.weforum.org/docs/WEF_Future_of_Jobs_2018.pdf; J. Lee. 2016. How can Asia Close Its Emerging Skills Gap? *World Economic Forum.* https://www.weforum.org/agenda/2016/01/how-can-asia-close-its-emerging-skills-gap.

(ii)   **Creating new flexible qualification pathways.** With almost 70% of the workforce not having graduated from senior secondary school, and one in every two workers deemed underqualified for their job, there is still some way to achieve lifelong learning in Indonesia—particularly in an era of rapidly changing technologies.[39] Beyond employment training centers targeted at individuals seeking work opportunities, more could be done to increase the general 4IR awareness of citizens through localized learning opportunities. Indonesia is starting to pursue some policies to include an 4IR focus within curricula. However, these are still relatively limited in scale and in the pilot or planning stage. In addition, the country still strongly emphasizes traditional qualifications attained through the education system or competency assessments, as opposed to past work experiences and the skills gained through them.

(iii)   **Building inclusiveness to extend the benefits of 4IR to underserved communities.** While 4IR could serve to bring about greater productivity and wealth, it could also exacerbate existing vulnerabilities certain segments of the labor market face, who may have less access to technological know-how. This is potentially a great source of risk in Indonesia, where labor market outcomes have been traditionally much poorer for women, youth, and rural workers.[40] There is limited evidence of strong government focus on building greater inclusiveness to allow underserved groups access to better opportunities in the labor market and train them in preparation for 4IR. Many of such programs seem to be undertaken by the private industry and nongovernment organizations. There is also a strong need to reenvision social protection mechanisms in the context of the advent of 4IR and the increasing number of on-demand or flexible workers—a rapidly rising segment of workers in Indonesia.

Assessment of Implementation of 4IR Policies ("The How")

Implementation of Indonesia's 4IR strategy for jobs and skills was assessed against three dimensions found to be crucial for success according to past academic work: the clarity and robustness of plans, strength of coordination between different stakeholders, and the alignment of financing and incentives (Figure 39).[41]

Indonesia's implementation road map for 4IR—which refers to its recently developed Making Indonesia 4.0 strategy—was assessed to be relatively robust. The strategy leads with a clearly articulated vision for 4IR, directs specific targets based on globally observed trends of the economic significance of 4IR and local data, and is the one shared road map that could be used across industry and government departments. Government financing is also strong in this area, particularly due to the emphasis placed on skills development. However, more can be done to put into action specific measures that link the country's employment and skills strategy across relevant government departments (e.g., Coordinating Ministry of Human Development and Cultural Affairs or CMHDCA), in coordination with industry and institutions. Stronger incentives may be needed for stakeholders to ensure that high quality training and education systems are observed. More specifically:

(i)   **Clarity and robustness of plans.** The starting point for successful 4IR implementation is to ensure there is a vision that is both realistic and clear, and skills policy is tightly integrated into the overall 4IR strategy. Indonesia's 4IR strategy has a clearly articulated vision and is robustly

39   *The Jakarta Post.* 2016. Five Plans to Upskill Indonesia's Workforce. https://www.thejakartapost.com/adv/2016/05/04/five-plans-to-upskill-indonesias-workforce.html; P. Rodrigo 2017. Half of All Indonesian Employees "May Be Underqualified." *CIPD.* https://www.cipd.asia/news/hr-news/half-indonesians-under-qualified.

40   ADB and OECD. 2015. *Education in Indonesia: Rising to the Challenge.* http://dx.doi.org/10.1787/9789264230750-en.

41   Based on AlphaBeta research of Industry 4.0 strategies, plus insights from past public industry research, including: M. Barber. 2007. *Instruction to Deliver: Fighting to Transform Britain's Public Services*; McKinsey & Company. 2012. *Delivery 2.0: The New Challenge for Governments.* https://www.mckinsey.com/industries/public-sector/our-insights/delivery-20-the-new-challenge-for-governments.

Figure 39: Implementation Challenges Associated with 4IR Policies for Jobs and Skills in Indonesia

Degree of current focus: | ■ Strong ■ Moderate ■ Weak

Dimension	Questions	Assessment
Clarity and robustness of plans	Is there a clearly articulated vision for 4IR?	Strong
	Is there strong integration between employment/skills and the 4IR plan?	Weak
	Is the plan forward looking, incorporating 4IR trends?	Strong
	Is there strong local data to support evidence-based policymaking?	Strong
Strengthening of coordination	Is there one shared road map across industry and government departments for 4IR?	Strong
	Is there coordination across different government ministries and levels?	Weak
	Is there strong alignment within and between industry and education or training institutions?	Moderate
Alignment of financing and incentives	Is government financing aligned with the strategic goals?	Moderate
	What are the strength of incentives for employers and workers to invest in skill development? What are the strength of incentives for teachers and institutions to ensure high-quality training and education systems?	Weak

4IR = Industry 4.0 or Fourth Industrial Revolution.

Note: Degree of focus was assessed based on the following criteria: "Strong" – few or no gaps between the country's policy implementation approach and approach seen in international best practices; "Moderate" – medium level of gaps between the country's policy implementation approach and approach seen in international best practices; and "Weak" – significant gaps between the country's policy implementation approach and approach seen in international best practices.

Source: Literature review; AlphaBeta analysis.

backed by local data, as well as studies on international trends in 4IR technology adoption and productivity benefits. However, there appears to be limited integration with the country's skills and employment strategy. Although the Making Indonesia 4.0 strategy spells out a priority of upgrading human capital, existing national employment and skills strategies by the CMHDCA need to concretely lay down initiatives to actualize this priority to develop the skillsets needed by 4IR.

(ii) **Strength of coordination between different stakeholders.** For skills and education programs to be effective in responding to 4IR, it is critical that all stakeholders are coordinated and aligned on these programs, their objectives, implementation mechanisms, and all related information. While the presence of one shared road map on 4IR in Indonesia is effective in aligning all government stakeholders on a common 4IR approach, the level of coordination between different ministries and levels of government in implementing this policy and integrating it with other relevant policies appears to be weak. Greater alignment is needed within and between industry and the training and education industries on the skills demanded and the training required to supply them. Recent initiatives to restructure the MENC and MORT need to consider strengthening such alignment with concrete action.

(iii) **Alignment of financing and incentives.** For jobs and skills policies to be successful in mitigating the potential negative impacts of 4IR, funding and incentives need to be well-aligned to ensure different stakeholders respectively contribute to skills development. While government financing is aligned with worker reskilling plans, incentives are weak for employers, teachers, training institutes, and even students to contribute toward skills development.

CHAPTER 4

The Way Forward

The three previous chapters highlighted a series of challenges facing Indonesia in relation to Industry 4.0 (4IR). This chapter summarizes those challenges and identifies several recommendations (based on relevant best practice in other countries) for how these could be addressed.

The COVID-19 Effect

The study was undertaken and completed prior to the spread of the coronavirus disease (COVID-19), which has caused unprecedented disruptions to labor markets and to the activities of the workforce across the world. This study's policy recommendations and strategies to strengthen widespread digital capabilities, enhance online/distance learning, digital platforms, education technology, and simulation-based learning have become all the more relevant in the aftermath of COVID-19. The key approaches discussed and elaborated in the report bear great relevance to the current context of countries experiencing nationwide closures of schools and training institutes. The expectation is also that post-COVID-19, there would be operating procedures that constitute a new normal that entails far more digital capabilities in the workplace. Hence, the findings of this study and the follow-on policy directions are timely and crucial for facilitating a sustainable COVID-19 recovery strategy.

The two sectors chosen for the study in Indonesia, F&B and automotive manufacturing sectors, have been adversely affected. In F&B, the expectation is that there would be lasting shifts in consumer behavior in dealing with the COVID-19 response. Food retailers are likely to scale up e-commerce. The logistics part of the sector in storing, transporting, and delivering is likely to become more tech-oriented, calling for new skills and talent. Similarly, in the auto industry, recovery after COVID-19 will entail embracing digital supply chains and launching digital sales and marketing initiatives. Hence, the upskilling and reskilling on 4IR-related occupations is even more urgent for the revival of the economy and economic stimulus needed in the post-COVID-19 era.

The study obviously does not address the implications of COVID-19 in Indonesia. However, the policy directions and future investments for higher order skills, particularly in the digital domain are eminently suitable for the country to reimagine new beginnings for the two sectors.

Recap of Industry 4.0-Related Challenges Facing Indonesia

Figure 40 provides a recap of the challenges facing Indonesia from the industry analysis (Chapter 1), the training institute survey (Chapter 2), and the policy assessment (Chapter 3).

Figure 40: Recap of Challenges Facing Indonesia in Relation to Industry 4.0

Area		Key challenges	Factoids
Sector-level analysis	1	Large displacement of workers in certain sectors, with large gender implications	Up to 29% of jobs could be displaced by 4IR technologies in the automotive industry
	2	Large shift in tasks and skill requirements	F&B industry workers could spend an additional ~14% of time on analytical and nonroutine interpersonal tasks
	3	Significant ramp up of on-the-job training, particularly for analytical skills	Roughly 50%-60% of new trainings related to 4IR will need to be delivered on-the-job
Training institute survey	4	Lack of robust quality certification processes for courses	75% of training institutions believe strengthening inspection and certification processes to be crucial
	5	Limited adoption of 4IR technologies in the classroom	Only 19% of training institutions are using virtual learning platforms
	6	Mismatch on skill expectations	96% of training institutions believe graduates to be adequately prepared for job market, but only only ~30% of employers agree
Policy assessment	7	Lack of flexible skill certification programs	Strong focus on traditional qualifications
	8	Lack of awareness of training opportunities	37% of workers stated that they did not know what courses to take for retraining
	9	Lack of incentives for investment by firms in worker training	4% more employers would rather hire new staff with the required skills than retrain existing workers
	10	Lack of inclusive skilling opportunities and social protection mechanisms for flexible workers	60% of employers are "very likely" to hire freelancers, but these workers are not covered by minimum wage guarantees, insurance, nor collective bargaining arrangements
	11	Lack of integrated 4IR and skills policy, and coordination between government departments	Indonesia's 4IR strategy has a clearly articulated vision but limited integration with the country's skills and employment strategy

4IR = Industry 4.0 or Fourth Industrial Revolution, F&B = food and beverage.
Source: Asian Development Bank and AlphaBeta.

Recommendations to Address Challenges

Indonesia could strengthen its approach to 4IR in a number of areas. Drawing upon international best practices related to the challenges highlighted above, several recommendations are outlined to strengthen Indonesia's approach in both policy scope and implementation processes (Table 3). For each recommendation, a series of steps or possible approaches are provided as a practical road map for implementation in Indonesia. Table 2 shows the key entity suggested to take the lead for each recommendation, as well as the other stakeholders to be involved. These entities span across the government, industry, education and training sectors, reflecting the importance of strong multi-stakeholder partnerships for implementing them.

Table 2: Suggested Leads and Stakeholders to Engage for Potential Actions in the Recommendations to Strengthen 4IR Approach

No.	Recommendation	Key Suggested Lead/s	Stakeholders to Involve
1	Develop 4IR transformation road maps for key sectors	Joint committee constituting the Coordinating Ministry of Economic Affairs and the Coordinating Ministry for Human Development and Cultural Affairs	• Constituent ministries of both coordinating ministries • Industry associations (including representatives from key employers in each sector) • Employer associations, • Training institutions, including BLKs • Higher education institutions
2	Develop a series of industry-led TVET programs targeting skills for 4IR	Industry associations	• Ministry of Manpower • Training institutions, including BLKs, • Higher education institutions • Senior high schools (SMKs)
3	Strengthen quality assurance mechanisms for training institutions	Ministry of Manpower and National Professional Certifications Board	• Training institutions, including BLKs, • Industry associations (including representatives from key companies with strong training programs in each sector)
4	Upgrade training delivery through 4IR technology in classrooms and training facilities	Ministry of Education and Culture	• Ministry of Research and Technology • Education technology ("edtech") companies
5	Develop flexible and modular skill certification programs	Ministry of Manpower	• Ministry of Education and Culture • Industry associations (including representatives from key companies with strong training programs in each sector), • Training institutions
6	Implement an incentive scheme for firms to train employees for 4IR	Ministry of Industry	• Industry associations (including representatives from key companies with strong training programs in each sector) • Training institutions, including BLKs
7	Formulate new approaches and measures to strengthen inclusion and social protection in the context of 4IR	Ministry of Manpower	• Employers of gig economy workers including companies that have established major sharing economy platforms (e.g., Grab, Go-Jek)

4IR = Industry 4.0 or Fourth Industrial Revolution, BLK = *Balai Latihan Kerja*, TVET = technical and vocational education and training.
Source: Asian Development Bank and AlphaBeta.

Table 3: Examples of 4IR Skills-Related Best Practices from Around the World

No	Recommendation	Common Challenges	Examples of Countries where Recommendation Implemented
1	Develop 4IR transformation road maps for key sectors	• Large displacement of workers in certain sectors, with large gender implications • Large shift in tasks and skill requirements • Lack of awareness of training opportunities • Lack of integrated 4IR and skills policy, and coordination between government departments	Australia, Singapore
2	Develop a series of industry-led TVET programs targeting skills for 4IR	• Mismatch on skill expectations • Significant ramp up of on-the-job training, particularly for analytical skills	Denmark, Finland, France, Germany, India, Norway, Switzerland
3	Strengthen quality assurance mechanisms for training institutions	• Lack of effective certification and quality assurance mechanisms in training	Australia, Ireland, Switzerland
4	Upgrade training delivery through 4IR technology in classrooms and training facilities	• Limited adoption of I4.0 technologies in the classroom	South Africa
5	Develop flexible and modular skill certification programs	• Lack of flexible skill certification programs	Malaysia
6	Implement an incentive scheme for firms to train employees for 4IR	• Lack of incentives for investment by firms in worker training	Malaysia, Singapore
7	Formulate new approaches and measures to strengthen inclusion and social protection in the context of 4IR	• Lack of inclusive skilling opportunities and social protection mechanisms for vulnerable workers	Australia, Japan, Malaysia, Republic of Korea

4IR = Industry 4.0 or Fourth Industrial Revolution, TVET = technical and vocational education and training.

Source: Asian Development Bank and AlphaBeta.

Recommendation 1: Develop Industry 4.0 transformation road maps for key sectors.

As noted in Chapter 3, Indonesia's 4IR strategy has a clearly articulated vision, and is robustly backed by local data and studies on international trends in 4IR technology adoption and productivity benefits. However, there is limited integration with the country's skills and employment strategy. Although the Making Indonesia 4.0 strategy has the priority of upgrading human capital, the Coordinating Ministry of Human Development and Cultural Affairs (CMHDCA) makes no reference to existing national employment and skills strategies, and how these would evolve to complement the skillsets 4IR needs. In addition, the Policy Road map on Vocational Education 2017–2025—though a product of coordination between the Coordinating Ministry of Economic Affairs (CMEA) with the Ministry of

Education and Culture (MENC) and the Ministry of Research and Technology (MORT)—does not have yet adequate detailed specification of skills required by future workers due to 4IR.[42]

A starting point to deepening coordination on 4IR skills development could be the development of industry-specific Industry Transformation Maps (ITMs), like in Singapore, which provide information on technology impacts, career pathways, the skills required for different occupations, and reskilling options (Box 7).[43] The development of these road maps could be led by a joint committee formed by the CMEA and the CMHDCA, and focus on Indonesia's automotive and F&B manufacturing industries for a start, and in particular, build on current efforts to synchronize skill needs by companies in both industries.

Box 7: Singapore's Industry Transformation Maps

Singapore's Industry 4.0 (4IR) effort, comprising the Industry Transformation Maps (ITMs), is championed by a dedicated body—the Future Economy Council (FEC). Chaired by the Deputy Prime Minister, the FEC is represented by members from the government, industry, unions, and educational and training institutes.[a] Each ITM represents the road map to 4IR technology adoption for an industry sector.[b] To ensure coordination and accountability within the government, a different government agency whose purview is most relevant to the sector champions each ITM (footnote b). For example, the Economic Development Agency leads the ITM for the manufacturing sector, while the Building and Construction Authority leads the built environment sector.

The Skills Framework is a key component of the ITMs. Co-created by industry, government, and civil society actors, the framework provides key information on career pathways, the existing and emerging skills required for different occupations, and reskilling options for different sectors. It also provides a list of training programs for skills upgrading. By virtue of its multi-stakeholder nature, this framework is also intended to benefit not just workers, but also employers (in enabling them to identify emerging skill needs for their workers and enhance talent attraction and retention efforts), training providers (in allowing them to gain better insights into emerging skill trains and more optimally target critical skill gaps through appropriate courses), and students (in facilitating them to make informed decisions on choice of study based on career aspirations). A 2018 survey of over 700 firms in Singapore found that 36% of firms take guidance from the ITMs on how to improve their talent pipeline, and how they could address manpower challenges for different sectors.[c]

4IR = Industry 4.0 or Fourth Industrial Revolution.

[a] Government of Singapore, Ministry of Trade and Industry. 2020. *The Future Economy Council.* https://www.mti.gov.sg/ FutureEconomy/TheFutureEconomyCouncil; Government of Singapore, Ministry of Education. 2016. *Formation of the Council for Skills, Innovation and Productivity.* https://www.moe.gov.sg/news/press-releases/formation-of-the-council-for-skills--innovation-and-productivity.

[b] Government of Singapore, Ministry of Trade and Industry. 2017. *Media Factsheet-Industry Transformation Maps.* https://www.mti.gov.sg/-/media/MTI/ITM/General/Fact-sheet-on-Industry-Transformation-Maps---revised-as-of-31-Mar-17.pdf.

[c] S. K. Tang. 2019. Singapore Businesses Not Investing Enough in Employee Training: SBF Survey. *Channel News Asia.* https://www.channelnewsasia.com/news/business/singapore-companies-not-investing-employee-training-sbf-survey-11134230.

Source: Asian Development Bank and AlphaBeta.

---

[42] International NGO Forum on Indonesian Development and Prakarsa. 2018. *Vokasi di era Revolusi Industry.* https://workequal. org/storage/app/uploads/public/5b7/fbb/d70/5b7fbbd7055d9469489896.pdf; International NGO Forum on Indonesian Development. 2018. *Policy Paper: Six Policy Recommendations on Vocational Training.* https://www.infid.org/wp-content/ uploads/2019/01/INFID-Policy-Paper-on-Decent-Work-web-1.pdf.

[43] SkillsFuture. 2019. *Skills Framework.* https://www.skillsfuture.sg/skills-framework.

This joint committee could be supported by industry associations (including companies with deeper experience in skills development such as Toyota in the automotive manufacturing sector), training institutions, and higher education institutes.

Recommendation 2: Develop a series of industry-led TVET programs targeting skills for Industry 4.0.

The poor quality of technical and vocational education and training (TVET) programs and their lack of industry relevance was identified in the employer surveys (in Chapter 1) and in the training institute survey (in Chapter 2). To strengthen the quality and relevance of TVET programs, it is recommended that Indonesia develop a series of industry-led TVET programs. This could build up on current industry efforts in Indonesia, such as Toyota's 2-year industry apprenticeship diploma program, and the Djarum Foundation's vocational schools, which offer practical courses on F&B processing techniques and technologies in laboratory environments.[44] While these have delivered significant results (e.g., an average of 75% of graduates from Toyota's diploma course are hired directly by the company each year), there is an opportunity for industry-led TVET programs to be scaled up to a larger scale with the government's support.

TVET programs could be led by industry associations, which could, in turn, work with the Ministry of Manpower (MOM) as well as training and educational institutions (in particular, senior high schools [SMKs], since many SMK leavers go on to undertake TVET training to access job opportunities) to scope them. Parameters to be designed include training curricula (including which 4IR technologies are to be taught) and their durations, teacher recruitment and training, and applicant criteria. In establishing the parameters of such programs, the formats observed in international best practices may be considered. Some notable examples include industry boot camps by McKinsey & Company's Generation program, which operates across several countries (Box 8).

Box 8: Connecting Students and Industry with Boot Camps

Industry needs appropriately trained recruits and youth job seekers need to be hired. Industry boot camps can help connect the skills offered by young job seekers to those needed by industry. The Generation Program develops programs focusing on four industries with teaching facilities in 119 cities in 6 continents. The program is offered to 18 to 29-year-olds.[a] Among the program's features are direct contact with potential employers; matching trainee attributes with employer needs; courses that cover technical, behavioral, and mental skills; continuous monitoring and support during and after the program; and a strong alumni network.

Since its inception, 31,600 people have gone through the training with 80% finding jobs within 3 months of finishing the program and 65% of those staying with their jobs for at least 1 year (footnote a). Employers also rate program graduates as higher-performing than their peers.[b]

[a]   Generation Program. 2019. https://www.generation.org/.
[b]   Asia Philanthropy Circle. 2017. *Catalysing Productive Livelihood: A Guide to Education Interventions with an Accelerated Path to Scale and Impact.* http://www.edumap-indonesia.asiaphilanthropycircle.org/wp-content/uploads/2017/11/APC-Giving-Guide-Book-Final-Report-17112017.pdf.

Source: Asian Development Bank and AlphaBeta.

---

44   Consultation with KADIN in July 2019; Djarum Foundation. 2019. *Vocational School Improvement Program, 2018–2019.*

Recommendation 3: Strengthen quality assurance mechanisms for training institutions.

In the survey of training institutions (Chapter 2), 75% of respondents highlighted quality assurance mechanisms as the most impactful area for policy intervention. The need for such mechanisms is also particularly important given that 46% of employers in the F&B manufacturing and 78% of those in automotive manufacturing industries reported large variations in the quality of vocational secondary graduates depending on region and education provider. In Indonesia, past reviews similarly highlighted concerns relating to the lack of qualified assessors, the lack of coordination between the three quality assurance institutions (with the result that the programs and objectives of the quality assurance institutions are not always in line), and the lack of involvement of the business community.[45]

Governments in countries across the world are also increasingly requiring evidence of a labor market need for new programs. This is the case for TVET programs in Australia, France, Hungary, Ireland, Poland, the Republic of Korea, Sweden, and the United States (US). Such labor market needs can be demonstrated in a variety of ways: for example, surveys reflecting the demand for specific training programs (Austria), employers' opinions (Denmark and Lithuania), agreements between educational institutions and employers to provide traineeship places (Hungary), and evidence of alignment with skills gap (Ireland). While the establishing of institution–industry partnerships highlighted earlier may help address some of the quality assurance concerns, it will also be important to understand the 4IR readiness of the quality assurance mechanisms in place in Indonesia, and to consider mechanisms to strengthen these approaches.

This initiative can be jointly led by the MOM, since it oversees all labor training efforts, and the National Professional Certifications Board. The quality assurance mechanisms can be scoped in tandem with training institutions themselves, and take into consideration feedback from industry (given their experience in recruiting graduates from the programs) on the parameters to consider when assessing the quality of various programs.

Recommendation 4: Upgrade training delivery through Industry 4.0 technology in classrooms and training facilities.

The survey of training institutions in Chapter 2 revealed that while many training institutions are using some technologies such as online learning modules, few are using other technologies such as virtual or augmented reality. The national stakeholder consultations in July and October 2019 also revealed varying levels of technology adoption across training institutions in Indonesia, with more well-resourced institutions having greater take-up of technologies.

There are a range of new technologies that could support 4IR instruction in Indonesia. Artificial intelligence (AI) technology, for example, is used to stimulate critical thinking by applying a virtual environment for building and assessing higher order inquiry skills.[46] AI-enabled immersive computer games is also used for science, technology, engineering, and math education in some schools in the US.[47] This is an area in which the MENC could take the lead in, and work with the MORT as well as education technology (EdTech) firms to incorporate 4IR technologies in classrooms from elementary schools

[45] UNESCO. 2017. *Towards Quality Assurance of Technical and Vocational Education and Training.* https://unesdoc.unesco.org/ark:/48223/pf0000259282.
[46] J. M. Spector and S. Ma. 2019. Inquiry and Critical Thinking Skills for the Next Generation: from Artificial Intelligence Back to Human Intelligence. *Smart Learning Environments Journal.* https://slejournal.springeropen.com/articles/10.1186/s40561-019-0088-z
[47] D. Ketelhut et al. 2009. A Multi-User Virtual Environment for Building and Assessing Higher Order Inquiry Skills in Science. *British Journal of Educational Technology.* https://onlinelibrary.wiley.com/doi/abs/10.1111/j.1467-8535.2009.01036.x.

Box 9: Leveraging Technologies to Improve Education and Address Gender Inequality

Digital technologies have been shown to improve education quality and even manage gender gaps starting from an early age.

The African School for Excellence, an affordable private secondary school in South Africa, deploys an innovative rotational classroom model in which students rotate between teacher-facilitated lessons, small-group peer-learning activities, and individual work on computers supervised by trainee teachers. Deploying online courses from free products such as Khan Academy, this blended learning approach innovatively reduces costs through its reliance on a smaller number of highly trained teachers, while enhancing education outcomes with its emphasis on personalized learning and small class sizes. Students in the African School for Excellence have been found to outperform the wealthiest students in the country by 2.3 times in mathematics and 1.4 times in English.[a] At the same time, the per-student cost of $800 a year is low when compared with South African averages that are in the range of $1,400 to $16,500 per year (footnote a).

Such personalized adaptive learning digital tools are also beginning to show their potential in bridging gender differences in students' attainment from a young age. A London-based nonprofit organization, "onebillion," focusing on building scalable educational software for children, launched the app "onecourse," which delivers content and practice on a tablet.[b] This app was found to prevent a gender gap in reading and mathematics skills from surfacing among first-grade students in Malawi—potentially by overcoming sociocultural factors responsible for gaps emerging in traditional classroom settings.[c]

[a] Center for Universal Education at Brookings. 2019. *Learning to Leapfrog: Innovative Pedagogies to Transform Education*. https://www.brookings.edu/wp-content/uploads/2019/09/Learning-to-Leapfrog-InnovativePedagogiestoTransformEducation-Web.pdf.
[b] onebillion. onecourse: One App that Delivers Reading, Writing and Numeracy. https://onebillion.org/onecourse/app/.
[c] Pathways for Prosperity Commission. 2019. *Positive Disruption: Health and Education in the Digital Age*. https://pathwayscommission.bsg.ox.ac.uk/positive-disruption.

Source: Asian Development Bank and AlphaBeta.

to universities and polytechnics. As installing such technologies and equipment at every institution could be fiscally challenging, a possible way to manage costs while maximizing their benefits is to adopt blended learning approaches. Such approaches combine both classroom and personalized online learning and have been demonstrated to be highly effective at not just improving education outcomes, but also addressing gender inequality (Box 9).

Recommendation 5: Develop flexible and modular skill certification programs.

As outlined in Chapter 3, traditional qualifications attained through the education system or competency assessments is still strongly emphasized. Thus, this recommendation encourages a stronger focus on skills—beyond such traditional qualifications—including in both the automotive and F&B manufacturing industries. The MOM could review current certification frameworks with the MENC to review the relative functions of educational qualifications and competency assessments arising from formal institutions and a more flexible approach for ongoing skills upgrading of workers with adequate recognition. This would involve (i) reviewing the need for minimum educational qualifications and competency-based assessments in current certification frameworks (with industry and training institutions); (ii) analyzing the potential impact of complementing or partially replacing such criteria with evidence of skills attainment from pathways, such as accredited training programs, industry

---

Box 10: The Malaysian Skills Certification Program

In Malaysia, individuals who do not possess formal educational qualifications have the opportunity to enter into their desired careers through the Malaysian Skills Certification Program.

Recognized by industry, this program awards Skills Certificates at five different levels:[a]

- (i) Malaysian Skills Certificate (SKM) Level 1
- (ii) Malaysian Skills Certificate (SKM) Level 2
- (iii) Malaysian Skills Certificate (SKM) Level 3
- (iv) Diploma in Skills Malaysia (DKM) Level 4
- (v) Malaysian Skills Advanced Diploma (DLKM) Level 5

These certificates are awarded across all industries of the economy—classified into 22 industries—according to the country's National Occupational Skills Standard.[b] Importantly, no former educational qualifications are required—the only requirements for candidates are the ability to speak and write in both Bahasa Melayu and English, and the need to pass a lower Skills Certificate level before qualifying for a higher level in the same field (note a).

Candidates may obtain these certificates through three channels: training in institutions accredited by the Jabatan Pembangunan Kemahiran (Department of Skills Development), industry apprenticeships under the National Dual Training System, and through sufficient Accreditation of Prior Achievement.[a] The third channel refers to accreditation gained through evidence of past work and/or training experience.

With these certificates being accredited as officially recognized qualifications and mapped to equivalent academic qualifications under the Malaysian Qualifications Framework, Malaysian companies are able to take guidance from this framework when assessing the suitability of job candidates without formal education, but who possess the relevant skills to excel at the job.[c]

[a] Government of Malaysia, Department of Skills Department. *Malaysian Skill Certificate (SKM)*. https://www.dsd.gov.my/index.php/en/service/malaysian-skills-certificate.
[b] OECD (2012), *Skills development pathways in Asia*. https://www.oecd.org/cfe/leed/Skills%20Development%20Pathways%20in%20Asia_FINAL%20VERSION.pdf.
[c] Government of Malaysia, Ministry of Higher Education and Malaysian Qualifications Agency. 2019. *Malaysian Qualifications Framework*. https://www.mqa.gov.my/pv4/mqf.cfm.

Source: Asian Development Bank and AlphaBeta.

---

apprenticeships, and certificates recognizing learning through past work experience (potentially taking reference from Malaysia's Skills Certification Framework, Box 10); and (iii) synchronizing these processes with the conventional certifications based on academic qualifications (ensuring they are recognized by employers).

Recommendation 6: Implement an incentive scheme for firms to train employees for Industry 4.0.

Despite the substantial productivity gains 4IR technologies could bring about (as demonstrated in Section 1), employer-led training efforts in Indonesia remain limited. Recent surveys reveal that less than a quarter of Indonesian companies conduct formal in-house training for their workers, and that 4% more employers would rather hire new staff with the required skills, as compared to those willing to retrain existing workers to attain these skills.[48] This low training rate could be explained by three key sources of market failure, which relate to both information asymmetries about the benefits and availability of training, as well as a lack of economic incentives for training:

(i)   There are information asymmetries pertaining to a limited awareness of the need for training in new digital skills. In a recent survey to understand the attitudes of Indonesian employers and their workers toward reskilling for AI, the most commonly cited reason (59% of employers and 45% of workers) for not undergoing training courses was there was insufficient time to do so, reflecting a lack of priority accorded to training.

(ii)   Another source of information asymmetry is the lack of awareness surrounding reskilling and reskilling opportunities. The same survey revealed that other key reasons for the inadequacy of training include a lack of awareness of which courses to take (37% of employers and 33% of workers), and the opinion that there were no suitable training programs (43% of employers and 23% of workers).[49]

(iii) Market-driven economic incentives for employer-led training efforts are weak due to a strong reliance on short-term contracting in the Indonesian labor market. This has led to underinvestment in training by companies and workers' lack of motivation (due to the absence of any foreseeable career progression) to invest in their own skills development.[50]

Given these, it is critical to develop a set of support programs to encourage firms to invest in relevant 4IR training for their workers. This action involves developing appropriate incentive programs for firms to invest in worker skill development related to 4IR. This action could be potentially led by the MOI in consultation with industry associations (including representatives from key companies with strong training programs in each sector) and training institutions, and done in four steps:

(i)   Identify appropriate incentive programs for firms (Box 11 provides some international examples);

(ii)   Undertake a holistic cost–benefit analysis of the incentive scheme and associated training programs (noting that cost–benefit analyses of skills training programs done from the government's perspective tend to focus largely on the direct economic costs of the program, while disregarding indirect economic benefits such as reduced welfare payments due to lower unemployment rates resulting from the training);

(iii) Pilot programs in a number of priority industries; and

(iv)   Scale the program to other industries, incorporating lessons learned from the pilot.

Recommendation 7: Formulate new approaches and measures to strengthen inclusion and social protection in the context of Industry 4.0.

With a substantial proportion of the population in low-income families and rural areas with few job opportunities as highlighted in Chapter 3, lifelong learning programs promoting inclusiveness in skills development in Indonesia is critical to ensure that the country's journey toward 4IR does not leave many

---

48   World Economic Forum. 2018. *The Future of Jobs Report 2018.* http://www3.weforum.org/docs/WEF_Future_of_Jobs_2018.pdf; J. W. Lee 2016. How can Asia Close its Emerging Skills Gap? *WEF Regional Agenda.* https://www.weforum.org/agenda/2016/01/how-can-asia-close-its-emerging-skills-gap.

49   Microsoft and IDC. 2019. *Microsoft – IDC Study: Artificial Intelligence to Nearly Double the Rate of Innovation in Asia Pacific by 2021.* https://news.microsoft.com/apac/2019/02/20/microsoft-idc-study-artificial-intelligence-to-nearly-double-the-rate-of-innovation-in-asia-pacific-by-2021/.

50   E. Allen. 2016. Emma Allen – Raising Indonesian labor productivity. *Nikkei Asian Review.* https://asia.nikkei.com/Economy/Emma-Allen-Raising-Indonesian-labor-productivity.

Box 11: Incentive Schemes for Firm Training in the Region

The Government of Singapore provides firm subsidies for employee training course fees and absentee payroll salary costs, with higher incentives awarded for government-certified courses.[a] For example, while subsidies for both government-certified and approved-certifiable courses cover 90% to 95% of course fees, those for approved-certifiable courses have hourly caps. On the other hand, the subsidies for noncertifiable courses are lower at SGD2 (~USD1.43) per hour of training. Absentee payroll funding is also accessible and covers up to 95% of hourly basic salary. The Government of Malaysia has a similar program, the Skills Upgrading Program, which provides grants covering 70% of training fees for small and medium-sized enterprises for technical and soft skills.[b]

[a] Skillsfuture Singapore. 2019. Funding Support for Employers. https://www.ssg.gov.sg/programmes-and-initiatives/funding/funding-for-employer-based-training.html.
[b] Microsoft and AlphaBeta. 2019. Preparing for AI: The Implications of Artificial Intelligence for Jobs and Skills In Asian Economies. https://news.microsoft.com/apac/2019/08/26/preparing-for-ai-the-implications-of-artificial-intelligence-for-jobs-and-skills-in-asian-economies.

Source: Asian Development Bank and AlphaBeta.

---

behind. The government is now preparing policies and commencing implementation of programs to enable underserved groups to access opportunities to train in preparation for 4IR. In developing targeted interventions, it is recommended that policy makers undertake an analysis to identify key vulnerable communities potentially facing the largest impact from 4IR, and work with relevant community leaders to scope targeted interventions. Possible approaches include providing access to online learning channels (e.g., the Ministry of Higher Education in Malaysia encourages and supports universities to create massive open online courses mandated to be made available to the public),[51] developing targeted skills development programs for specific underserved groups, and providing financial incentives for employers to train specific underserved communities (e.g., the Career-up Josei-kin program in Japan provides employers with subsidies for training individuals on nonregular contracts).[52]

The Ministry of Social Affairs is piloting initiatives for productive inclusion by linking social assistance programs with entrepreneurship grants and opportunities for skills development. These are promising and can also be further explored in the context of 4IR.

The lack of social protection policies for Indonesia's rapidly growing on-demand workers is highlighted in Chapter 3 as one of the key concerns seeing the least amount of focus in Indonesia's current policy context. This is significant given the large number and continued growth of these workers. For example, it was found that on-demand ride-hailing drivers in Indonesia grew rapidly from less than 100 drivers in 2010 to over 1 million drivers in 2018.[53] It was also found that even though many of these drivers benefited from increased job opportunities and higher incomes, they also work up to 13 hours per day, exceeding the legal maximum of 8 hours.[54] Yet, they are not covered by minimum wage guarantees,

---

[51] UNESCO. 2017. *Lifelong Learning in Transformation: Promising Practices in Southeast Asia.* https://unesdoc.unesco.org/ark:/48223/pf0000253603.
[52] OECD. 2017. *Financial Incentives for Steering Education and Training, Getting Skills right.* https://www.skillsforemployment.org/edmsp1/groups/skills/documents/skpcontent/ddrf/mtg5/~edisp/wcmstest4_189496.pdf.
[53] GoJek. https://www.gojek.com/sg/about/.
[54] N. Harsono. 2019. Experts Take on Protecting Rapidly Growing Number of Gig Workers. *The Jakarta Post.* https://www.thejakartapost.com/news/2019/07/24/experts-take-on-protecting-rapidly-growing-number-of-gig-workers.html.

insurance, nor collective bargaining arrangements. Demand for on-demand workers in other industries is also high; a survey found that 60% of employers across different industries in Indonesia are "very likely" to hire freelancers to address skill gaps.[55] It is recommended that the MOM undertake feasibility analyses of several policy options for the social protection of these workers. These options could include:

(i) **Enhancing the income security for on-demand workers through government policy.** Some international best practices in this area could be considered. For example, in Australia, workers on short-term contracts are entitled to an increment of 25% for each hour worked compared to a worker doing the same job on an ongoing basis.[56] These workers also benefit from minimum-hour guarantees—employers have to pay them for at least 3 hours of work each time they engage their services.

(ii) **Work with key employers to champion corporate policies mandating income stability for on-demand workers.** Given that the use of on-demand labor has been demonstrated to reduce labor costs for firms—a study found that 43% of global organizations engaging such labor saved at least 20% in labor costs. There is much scope for companies to develop policies that mandate the income stability for on-demand workers, such as minimum pay, without incurring higher net labor costs.[57] In the absence of established regulation in this area, the Government of Indonesia could work with key employers to develop corporate policies to mandate the income stability of these workers, and establish them as local champions that other companies could model on. For example, the multinational technology company Microsoft has an established policy for on-demand workers, which includes minimum pay requirements and a stipulation that all these workers must be paid within 1 week of completion of the work.[58]

(iii) **Work with existing online job or sharing economy platforms to mandate social security contributions for on-demand workers.** The government could consider working with key sharing economy platforms in the country (e.g., Grab and GoJek) to provide for mandatory social security contributions.[59] Such contributions could come from either or both companies, and their customers. For example, Care.com is a platform for caregivers seeking work, enables families seeking such services (the customers) to contribute to their caregiver's benefits similar to how traditional corporate employers fund employee benefits.[60] A strong government push for similar measures implemented in other platforms could be effective in creating stronger safety nets for the country's on-demand workers.

Industry-Specific Priorities

While these recommendations apply to both the F&B and automotive manufacturing industries, there are a set of priorities unique to each industry that should be considered when implementing the respective actions. Aimed at tackling the underlying weaknesses in each industry's ability to reap the benefits from 4IR technologies, these priorities were formed based on the findings in the earlier sections, as well as by in-country consultations with government, industry, and training and education sector stakeholders.

[55] World Economic Forum. 2018. *The Future of Jobs Report 2018.* https://www.weforum.org/reports/the-future-of-jobs-report-2018.

[56] OECD. 2018/ *The Future of Social Protection: What Works for Non-Standard Workers?* https://doi.org/10.1787/9789264306943-en.

[57] KellyOCG. 2018. *From Workforce to Workfit.* https://www.kellyocg.com/insights/featured-content/whitepapers/from-workforce-to-workfit/.

[58] Microsoft. 2018. *The Future Computed.* https://blogs.microsoft.com/wp-content/uploads/2018/02/The-Future-Computed_2.8.18.pdf.

[59] L. Hasnan 2019. Philippines' Fast-Growing Gig Economy. *The ASEAN Post.* https://theaseanpost.com/article/philippines-fast-growing-gig-economy.

[60] G. Bonoli. 2019. Ensuring Economic Security in the Gig Economy. *The Business Times.* https://www.businesstimes.com.sg/opinion/ensuring-economic-security-in-the-gig-economy; Microsoft. 2018. *The Future Computed.* https://blogs.microsoft.com/wp-content/uploads/2018/02/The-Future-Computed_2.8.18.pdf.

Food and Beverage Manufacturing Industry

- **Improve the quality of industry-relevant education and training courses to ensure stronger alignment with the skills demanded by employers.** With the employer survey revealing that a third of employers in this industry believe that fresh graduates are inadequately prepared by their pre-hire education and/or training institutions, there is an urgent need for a targeted assessment of the areas in which employers believe graduates fall short, and identify potential drivers for this based on a review of current curriculums and teaching pedagogies. An industry-focused suite of courses serving all levels of the workforce could be considered in response to the strategic role this sector has for the country's global competitiveness.

- **Address relative lack of private sector support for 4IR adoption and skills training.** Owing to its large MSME composition, consultation with the CMEA reflected that this sector receives relatively less support from the private sector in terms of 4IR skills training—as compared to the automotive manufacturing industry where there are a number of large players with more established know-how and systems for 4IR adoption. This industry could thus benefit from a stronger emphasis on government-led policies (e.g., Recommendation 1 on 4IR transformation road map and skilling framework; Recommendation 3 on quality assurance mechanisms; and Recommendation 5 on skill certification programs). Exploring the economic dimensions of downstream services sector linkages (such as restaurants and related businesses) would also be productive.

- **Prioritize 4IR technologies and skill sets that could address large postharvest losses.** A key and urgent objective of undertaking 4IR stated by industry stakeholders was to tackle the country's substantial postharvest losses that amounted to as much as 15% per year. In scoping the type of technology to be adopted and the corresponding skills development programs, it is thus important to prioritize the technologies and relevant know-how that could help address this issue (e.g., the development of Internet of Things-enabled tracking devices for food stocks transiting through the supply chain), and also incorporate training and awareness-raising initiatives to deploy these technologies cost-effectively.

Automotive Manufacturing Industry

- **Prioritize 4IR adoption and related skills development efforts for MSMEs.** Consultation with local industry stakeholders revealed a significant gap in 4IR technology adoption and skilling rates between large, multinational companies, and MSMEs in the industry.[61] The analysis in Chapter 1 similarly reflected that although 70% of enterprises in the industry are MSMEs focused on producing and supplying parts to large manufacturers, there are blind spots of unmet skilling needs in these small parts manufacturing businesses. It is thus recommended that adequate focus be placed on MSMEs when implementing the specific policy recommendations (e.g., allocating resources for skills development programs such as industry-led TVET programs, MSME-relevant skills transformation road maps).

- **Support 4IR knowledge transfer from large multinational companies to MSMEs.** Indonesia's automotive manufacturing industry is an ecosystem consisting of a number of large car assembly companies (typically multinational companies with entities established locally in the country), and small and medium-sized small components and parts manufacturing companies that act as suppliers to the large companies. Being more well-resourced and with stronger international networks, these large companies are generally in a more advanced stage of 4IR adoption and training than MSMEs, and some have posted positive results from their skills programs. Several, such as Toyota and Honda for example, even have full-fledged training institutes and apprenticeship programs. There is thus a compelling push for there to be knowledge transfer on

---

[61]   Based on consultations with automotive manufacturing industry stakeholders in October 2019.

4IR adoption and skills development strategies from these large companies to MSMEs. These large companies can also be instrumental to supporting many of the policy recommendations outlined—from formulating the 4IR transformation road maps for the automotive manufacturing industry (Recommendation 1) to co-creating the skill certification programs for the industry (Recommendation 5) that MSMEs can then take reference from and incorporate into their own training programs. Where the required competencies overlap, there could even be scope for consolidated training programs led by these large companies for the benefit of MSMEs.

- **Foster stronger coordination between BLKs and individual company-led training institutes.** While both groups are already leading significant skills development efforts for the industry, there was a strong sentiment reflected by national consultations of a lack of knowledge-sharing between *Balai Latihan Kerjas* (BLKs) and individual company-led training institutes (e.g., Toyota and Honda Polytechnics). Both sets of institutions had also developed and adhered largely to their own skills standards, resulting in diverse set of skilling standards and practices that may be incoherent. Fostering stronger coordination between both groups is thus critical to ensuring that workers in this industry are held to the same and easily recognizable standards that serve as benchmarks.

With the Asian Development Bank, the AlphaBeta team consulted a range of government and industry stakeholders in a series of initial consultations in July 2019, and through a workshop in October 2019. The lists of stakeholders consulted in both engagements are provided in Tables A1 and A2.

Table A1: Stakeholders Engaged in Initial Consultations in July 2019

Entity	Stakeholders Engaged
Government Agencies	
Ministry of Industry	• Eko Cahyanto, Head of Industrial R&D Agency • Mujiyono, Head of Center for Education and Training, and Coordinator of Vocational Education • Setyoko Pramono, Head of Division for Industrial Vocational Education Development, Agency of Industrial Human Resource Development
Ministry of Education and Culture	• Ananto Kusuma Seta, Senior Advisor to the Minister for Innovation and Competitiveness • Sulistio Mukti Cahyono, Head of Vocational Alignment, Sub-directorate of Vocational Alignment and Industrial Partnership
Ministry of Research and Technology (formerly known as Ministry of Research, Technology and Higher Education)	• Patdono Suwignjo, Director General of Science, Technology and Higher Education Institution • Ismunandar, Secretary General and Director General of Learning and Student Affairs
Ministry of Manpower	• Gilang Amaldi, Head of the Data and Information Department under the Program, Evaluation, and Reporting Section • Muchtar Azis, Directorate of Competency Standard and Training Development under the Directorate General of Training and Productivity Development
Coordinating Ministry for Economic Affairs	• Yulius Ibnoe, Director for Manpower
Industry Associations	
KADIN / APINDO	• Bob Azam, Head of the Standing Committee on Employment Training • Anton Supit, Vice Chairman for the Field of Employment and Industrial Relations • Afien Wibhawa, Member, National Vocational Training Committee • Henrik Kuffner, Advisor

continued on next page

Table A1 *continued*

Entity	Stakeholders Engaged
Education and Training Institutes	
State Polytechnic of Jakarta	• Iwan Supriyadi, Secretary 2, Student Affairs and Industrial Relations • Riandini and Saamaryarni, Electrical and Electronic Engineering Lecturers
Nongovernment Organizations	
Djarum Foundation	• Primadi Serad, Program Director

Source: Asian Development Bank and AlphaBeta.

Table A2: Stakeholders Engaged in Country Workshop in October 2019

Entity	Stakeholders Engaged
Government Agencies	
Ministry of Research and Technology (formerly known as Ministry of Research, Technology and Higher Education)	• Afriyudianto, Head of Section, Directorate of Learning, Directorate General of Learning and Student Affairs, Ministry of Research, Technology and Higher Education • Dewi W – Directorate General of Learning and Student Affairs
BAPPENAS	• Teguh Sambodo, Director of Industry, Tourism, and Creative Economy • Mahatmi Parwitasari Saronto, Director for Manpower and Employment Expansion • Yeni Febriyani, Directorate of TKPKK • Dimas, Secretariat General of Science, Technology and Higher Education Institutions • Mochamad Eldg NM, Dit. TKPKK • M. Iqbal Abbas
Coordinating Ministry for Economic Affairs	• Agus Salim, Head of Competency Certification and international Cooperation Subdivision
Ministry of Education and Culture	• Devi Istiya • Sulistio MC • Muktiono Waspodo • Nur. Hanifah • Qori Syahrrana
Ministry of Finance	• Fikraus • Antoni Siomtuyi • I Gede Awan Sastra Winaya, Head of Information Technology Directorate General of Financing and Risk Management
Ministry of Manpower	• Sukiyo, Director of Competency and Training Development • Moh. Syikhab, Head of Data and Information Development • Siswantari, Secretary of the Director General of Pelitihan and Productivity

continued on next page

Table A2 *continued*

Entity	Stakeholders Engaged
Industry	
KADIN	• Subchan Gatot, Vice Chairman • Henrik Kuffner, Advisor
PT Toyota Motor Manufacturing Indonesia	• Daniel S., General Manager
ZebraX	• Akhmad Sani, Senior Consultant
Education and Training Institutes	
State Polyteknik Jakarta	• Nunung Martina, Head of P3AI and Head of Senate Commission 1 • Iwan Supriyadi, Secretary 2, Student Affairs and Industrial Relations

TKPKK = *Tenaga Kerja dan Perluasan Kesempatan Kerja* (Directorate of manpower and expansion of job opportunities).

Source: Asian Development Bank and AlphaBeta.

Bibliography

ACT/EMP and ILO. 2017. ASEAN in Transformation: How Technology is Changing Jobs and Enterprises: Indonesia Country Brief. https://www.ilo.org/wcmsp5/groups/public/---ed_dialogue/---act_emp/documents/publication/wcms_579671.pdf.

Asian Development Bank (ADB). 2013. *Technological Change, Skill Demand, and Wage Inequality in Indonesia.* https://www.adb.org/publications/technological-change-skill-demand-and-wage-inequality-indonesia.

ADB. 2018. *Asian Development Outlook 2018: How Technology Affects Jobs.* https://www.adb.org/publications/asian-development-outlook-2018-how-technology-affects-jobs.

ADB-BAPPENAS. 2019. *Policies to Support the Development of Indonesia's Manufacturing Industry during 2020–2024.* https://www.adb.org/publications/policies-manufacturing-sector-indonesia-2020-2024.

ADB and OECD. 2015. *Education in Indonesia: Rising to the Challenge.* http://dx.doi.org/10.1787/9789264230750-en.

Allen, E. R. 2016. Raising Indonesian Labor Productivity. *Nikkei Asian Review.* https://asia.nikkei.com/Economy/Emma-Allen-Raising-Indonesian-labor-productivity.

Asia Philanthropy Circle. 2017. Catalysing Productive Livelihood: A Guide to Education Interventions with an Accelerated Path to Scale and Impact. https://www.edumap-indonesia.asiaphilanthropycircle.org/.

Barber, M. 2007. *Instruction to Deliver: Fighting to Transform Britain's Public Services.* https://www.amazon.com/Instruction-Deliver-Michael-Barber/dp/0413776646.

The Behavioural Insights Team, Cabinet Office and Nesta. 2015. Easy, Attractive, Timely, Social: Four Simple Ways to Apply Behavioural Insights. https://www.behaviouralinsights.co.uk/wp-content/uploads/2015/07/BIT-Publication-EAST_FA_WEB.pdf.

Bonoli, G. 2019. Ensuring Economic Security in the Gig Economy. *The Business Times.* https://www.businesstimes.com.sg/opinion/ensuring-economic-security-in-the-gig-economy.

Boston Consulting Group. 2015. *Industry 4.0: The Future of Productivity and Growth in Manufacturing Industries.* https://www.bcg.com/publications/2015/engineered_products_project_business_industry_4_future_productivity_growth_manufacturing_industries.

Center for Universal Education at Brookings Institution. 2019. Learning to Leapfrog: Innovative Pedagogies to Transform Education. https://www.brookings.edu/wp-content/uploads/2019/09/Learning-to-Leapfrog-Policy-Brief-Web.pdf.

Deloitte. 2015. 3D Opportunity Serves it Up: Additive Manufacturing and Food. https://www2.deloitte.com/us/en/insights/focus/3d-opportunity/3d-printing-in-the-food-industry.html.

Generation Program. 2019. https://www.generation.org/.

Goehrke, S. 2018. Additive Manufacturing is Driving the Future of the Automotive Manufacturing Industry. *Forbes.* https://www.forbes.com/sites/sarahgoehrke/2018/12/05/additive-manufacturing-is-driving-the-future-of-the-automotiveindustry/#2eb708e775cc.

Government of Indonesia, Ministry of Industry. 2018. *Making Indonesia 4.0.* http://www.kemenperin.go.id/kebijakan-industri.

———. 2015. *National Industrial Development Master Plan 2015–2035.* https://kemenperin.go.id/ripin.pdf.

———. 2010. National Medium-Term Industrial Development Plan 2015–2019. http://www.kemenperin.go.id/profil/71/rencana-strategiskementerian-perindustrian.

Government of Indonesia, Ministry of Manpower. 2019. *Penandatanganan Kerja Sama "BLK" Komunitas Tahap I Tahun 2019 antara Kementerian Ketenagakerjaan dengan Lembaga Penerima Bantuan.* https://www.kemenkumham.go.id/publikasi/siaran-pers/penandatanganan-kerja-sama-blk-komunitas-tahap-i-tahun-2019-antara-kementerian-ketenagakerjaan-dengan-lembaga-penerima-bantuan.

Government of Indonesia, Ministry of Research and Technology. 2019. *Policies and Programs.* https://international.ristekdikti.go.id/policies-and-programs/.

Government of Indonesia, Sekretariat Kabinet Republik Indonesia. 2016. *Presidential Decree No. 9 Year 2016 on "Revitalizing SMKs to Improve the Quality and Competitiveness of Indonesian Human Resources."* https://kemdikbud.go.id/main/files/download/e451d9ec3a04121.

Government of Malaysia, Department of Skills Development. *Malaysian Skill Certificate (SKM).* https://www.dsd.gov.my/index.php/en/service/malaysian-skills-certificate.

Government of Malaysia, Ministry of Higher Education and Malaysian Qualifications Agency. 2017. *Malaysian Qualifications Framework (MQF) 2nd edition.* https://www.mqa.gov.my/pv4/document/mqf/2019/Oct/updated%20MQF%20Ed%202%2024102019.pdf.

Government of Malaysia, Ministry of Higher Education and Malaysian Qualifications Agency. 2011. *Malaysian Qualifications Framework.* https://www.mqa.gov.my/pv4/mqf.cfm.

Government of Singapore, Ministry of Education. 2016. Formation of the Council for Skills, Innovation and Productivity. https://www.moe.gov.sg/news/press-releases/formation-of-the-council-for-skills--innovation-and-productivity.

Government of Singapore, Ministry of Trade and Industry. 2017. *Media Factsheet: Industry Transformation Maps.* https://www.mti.gov.sg/-/media/MTI/ITM/General/Fact-sheet-on-Industry-Transformation-Maps---revised-as-of-31-Mar-17.pdf.

Hasnan, L. 2019. Philippines' Fast-Growing Gig Economy. *The ASEAN Post.* https://theaseanpost.com/article/philippines-fast-growing-gig-economy.

International Labour Organization. 2018. Improving *Practical Skills of Job Seekers through Apprenticeship.* https://www.ilo.org/jakarta/info/public/pr/WCMS_636126/lang--en/index.htm.

Indonesia Investments. 2018. Widodo Launches Road map for Industry 4.0: "Making Indonesia 4.0." https://www.indonesia-investments.com/business/business-columns/widodo-launches-roadmap-for-industry-4.0-making-indonesia-4.0/item8711.

International Federation of Robotics. 2019. Why Robot Sales in China will Survive Slowdown in Car Production. https://ifr.org/post/Why-robot-sales-in-China-will-survive-slowdown-in-car-production.

The Jakarta Post. Five Plans to Upskill Indonesia's Workforce. 2016. https://www.thejakartapost.com/adv/2016/05/04/five-plans-to-upskill-indonesias-workforce.html.

KellyOCG. 2018. From Workforce to Workfit. https://www.kellyocg.com/insights/featured-content/whitepapers/from-workforce-to-workfit/.

Ketelhut, D. et al. 2009. A Multi-user Virtual Environment for Building and Assessing Higher Order Inquiry Skills in Science. *British Journal of Educational Technology.* https://onlinelibrary.wiley.com/doi/abs/10.1111/j.1467-8535.2009.01036.x.

Lee, J. 2016. How Can Asia Close its Emerging Skills Gap? *World Economic Forum.* https://www.weforum.org/agenda/2016/01/how-can-asia-close-its-emerging-skills-gap.

Lewandowski, P. et al. 2019. Technology, Skills and Globalization: Explaining International Differences in Routine and Non-routine Work using Survey Data. *IBS working paper.* April 2019. https://ibs.org.pl/en/publications/technology-skills-and-globalization-explaining-international-differences-in-routine-and-nonroutine-work-using-survey-data/.

Masters, K. 2015. The Impact of Industry 4.0 on the Automotive Manufacturing Industry. https://blog.flexis.com/the-impact-of-industry-4.0-on-the-automotive-industry.

Arbulu, I. et al. 2018. *Industry 4.0: Reinvigorating ASEAN Manufacturing for the Future.* McKinsey & Company. 8 February. https://www.mckinsey.com/business-functions/operations/our-insights/industry-4-0-reinvigorating-asean-manufacturing-for-the-future.

Daly, E. and S. Singham. 2012. Delivery 2.0: The New Challenge for Governments. *McKinsey & Company.* 1 September. https://www.mckinsey.com/industries/public-and-social-sector/our-insights/delivery-20-the-new-challenge-for-governments.

Woetzl, J. et al. 2014. *Southeast Asia at the Crossroads: Three Paths to Prosperity.* McKinsey Global Institute. November. https://www.mckinsey.com/~/media/McKinsey/Featured%20Insights/Asia%20Pacific/Three%20paths%20to%20sustained%20economic%20growth%20in%20Southeast%20Asia/MGI%20SE%20Asia_Executive%20summary_November%202014.ashx.

Microsoft. 2018. *The Future Computed.* https://blogs.microsoft.com/wp-content/uploads/2018/02/The-Future-Computed_2.8.18.pdf.

Microsoft. 2018. Microsoft–IDC Study: Artificial Intelligence to Nearly Double the Rate of Innovation in Asia Pacific by 2021. https://news.microsoft.com/apac/2019/02/20/microsoft-idc-study-artificial-intelligence-to-nearly-double-the-rate-of-innovation-in-asia-pacific-by-2021/.

Microsoft. 2019. *Preparing for AI: The implications of Artificial Intelligence for Jobs and Skills in Asian Economies.* 26 August. https://news.microsoft.com/apac/2019/08/26/preparing-for-ai-the-implications-of-artificial-intelligence-for-jobs-and-skills-in-asian-economies/.

Organisation for Economic Co-operation and Development (OECD). 2018. *The Future of Social Protection: What Works for Non-Standard Workers?* https://doi.org/10.1787/9789264306943-en.

OECD. 2012. *Skills Development Pathways in Asia.* https://www.oecd.org/cfe/leed/Skills%20Development%20Pathways%20in%20Asia_FINAL%20VERSION.pdf.

OECD. 2010. *Learning for Jobs: The OECD International Survey of VET Systems: First Results and Technical Report.* https://www.oecd.org/education/skills-beyond-school/47334855.pdf.

onebillion. *onecourse: One App that Delivers Reading, Writing and Numeracy.* https://onebillion.org/onecourse/app/.

Oxford Economics. 2018. Technology and the Future of ASEAN Jobs. https://www.oxfordeconomics.com/recent-releases/dd577680-7297-4677-aa8f-450da197e132.

Pathways for Prosperity Commission. 2019. *Positive Disruption: Health and Education in the Digital Age.* https://pathwayscommission.bsg.ox.ac.uk/positive-disruption.

Prospera and AlphaBeta Advisors. 2019. *Capturing Indonesia's Automation Potential.* https://www.alphabeta.com/wp-content/uploads/2019/08/capturing-indonesias-automation-potential.pdf.

RAND. 2018. *Indonesian Family Life Survey (IFLS).* https://www.rand.org/well-being/social-and-behavioral-policy/data/FLS/IFLS.html.

Rodrigo, P. 2017. Half of All Indonesian Employees "May Be Underqualified." *CIPD.* https://www.cipd.asia/news/hr-news/half-indonesians-under-qualified.

Schwab, K. 2017. *The Fourth Industrial Revolution.* https://books.google.com.sg/books?hl=en&lr=&id=ST_FDAAAQBAJ&oi=fnd&pg=PR7&dq=klaus+schwab+fourth+industrial+revolution&ots=DTnvbTqvTQ&sig=aOLqcUCFsLKbNpjWa5kr2Sjzhu4#v=onepage&q=klaus%20schwab%20fourth%20industrial%20revolution&f=false.

SkillsFuture Singapore. 2019. *Funding Support for Employers.* https://www.ssg.gov.sg/programmes-and-initiatives/funding/funding-for-employer-based-training.html.

———. 2019. *Skills Framework.* https://www.skillsfuture.sg/skills-framework.

Spector, J. M. and S. Ma. 2019. Inquiry and Critical Thinking Skills for the Next Generation: from Artificial Intelligence Back to Human Intelligence. *Smart Learning Environments Journal.* 6 (8). https://slejournal.springeropen.com/articles/10.1186/s40561-019-0088-z.

Sullivan, R. 2019. Increased Role of Robots in Food Manufacturing. *Food Quality & Safety.* 25 February. https://www.foodqualityandsafety.com/article/increased-role-of-robots-in-food-manufacturing/.

Tang, S. K. 2019. Singapore Businesses Not Investing Enough in Employee Training: SBF Survey. *Channel News Asia.* https://www.channelnewsasia.com/news/business/singaporecompanies-not-investing-employee-training-sbf-survey-11134230.

United Nations Educational, Scientific and Cultural Organization. 2017. Towards Quality Assurance of Technical and Vocational Education and Training. https://unesdoc.unesco.org/ark:/48223/pf0000259282.

U.S. Agency for International Development and Family Health International 360. 2015. Workforce Connections: Analysis of Skills Demand in Indonesia. https://www.fhi360.org/sites/default/files/media/documents/resource-skills-analysis-indonesia.pdf.

VarInsights. 2010. YCH Group Selects Intermec Fixed Vehicle Computer to Improve Supply Chain Management. https://www.varinsights.com/doc/ych-group-selects-intermec-fixed-vehicle-0004.

World Bank and AT Kearney. 2018. *Readiness for the Future of Production Report 2018.* http://www3.weforum.org/docs/FOP_Readiness_Report_2018.pdf.

World Economic Forum (WEF). 2019. Towards a Reskilling Revolution: Industry-Led Action for the Future of Work. http://www3.weforum.org/docs/WEF_Towards_a_Reskilling_Revolution.pdf.

WEF. 2018. *The Future of Jobs Report 2018.* http://www3.weforum.org/docs/WEF_Future_of_Jobs_2018.pdf.